ROBOT CONTROL

Edited by **Efrén Gorrostieta Hurtado**

Robot Control
http://dx.doi.org/10.5772/61728
Edited by Efrén Gorrostieta Hurtado

Contributors

Tadej Petrič, Miha Deniša, Andrej Gams, Ales Ude, Marcos Batista Figueredo, Mauro Bellone, Edgar Alonso Martínez García, Gerson Santos-Medina, Karla Heras-Gaytan, Rafael Torres-Córdoba, Victor Carrillo-Saucedo, Dora Luz Almanza Ojeda, Yazmin Gomar-Vera, Mario-Alberto Ibarra-Manzano, Mariam Al-Sagban

Published by InTech

Janeza Trdine 9, 51000 Rijeka, Croatia

Publishing Process Manager Andrea Koric

Technical Editor SPi Global

Cover InTech Design team

First published September, 2016

Printed in Croatia

Additional hard copies can be obtained from orders@intechopen.com

Robot Control, Edited by Efrén Gorrostieta Hurtado

p. cm.

Print ISBN 978-953-51-2684-3

Online ISBN 978-953-51-2685-0

For EU product safety concerns:
IN TECH d.o.o., Prolaz Marije Krucifikse Kozulić 3, 51000 Rijeka, Croatia,
info@intechopen.com or visit our website at intechopen.com.

Meet the editor

Dr. Eng Efren Gorrostieta is a Professor at the Engineering Faculty of the Autonomous University of Queretaro, Mexico. He studied Electronics Engineering, received a master of Science in Control and Automation and a PhD in Mechatronics. He was a co-founder of the Mechatronics Mexican Association, President of the IEEE Querétaro Section and the Chair of the IEEE Queretaro Computational Intelligence Chapter; he has given lectures in Control Systems and Robotics at different universities and has been a chair, reviewer and editor in several national/international congresses related to robotics, automation, and artificial intelligence. He has several publications in conferences and journals in the field.

Contents

Preface

One of the topics of interest and technical development is the automatic control system research. From the beginning, it has been a growing booster of different knowledge areas. Remember, for example, first developments such as the water clocks and the watt regulator that helped at that time with the development of the industrial revolution.

Along the history, we can find different mathematical tools that have allowed the development of single-input single-output (SISO) control systems, which demanded a certain degree of knowledge in the feedback systems in contrast to the multivariable systems, modeling and physical representation, stability concepts, observability and regulator design, etc., of today.

In case of robotic development, we consider multivariable control systems, where each of the variables must follow the instructions of the kinematic control with the aim of trajectory following in which each of the joint movements must be required to comply the specific tasks.

This book contains a selection of research works focused on robot control applications where the reader can appreciate the development and progress of these systems. There are descriptions of projects in each section in areas such as mobile robotics, navigation systems, trajectory-planning navigation systems, and non-holonomic systems.

On the other hand, one of the areas of knowledge that has been developed and that eventually helped the development of robotic control is without doubt artificial intelligence. In this book, we will find control schemes for robotics using artificial intelligence concepts in order to face highly non-linear systems.

The editor specially appreciates and thanks authors of the chapters who shared their knowledge with the scientific community and other potential readers.

Dr. Eng. Efrén Gorrostieta
Engineering Faculty of the Autonomous University of Querétaro
Cerros de las Campanas
Queretaro Qro
Mexico

Chapter 1

A Review of Compliant Movement Primitives

Miha Deniša, Tadej Petrič, Andrej Gams and
Aleš Ude

Additional information is available at the end of the chapter

http://dx.doi.org/10.5772/64058

Abstract

Dynamical models of robots performing tasks in contact with objects or the environment are difficult to obtain. Therefore, different methods of learning the dynamics of tasks have been proposed. In this chapter, we present a method that provides the joint torques needed to execute a task in a compliant and at the same time accurate manner. The presented method of compliant movement primitives (CMPs), which consists of the task kinematical and dynamical trajectories, goes beyond mere reproduction of previously learned motions. Using statistical generalization, the method allows to generate new, previously untrained trajectories. Furthermore, the use of transition graphs allows us to combine parts of previously learned motions and thus generate new ones. In the chapter, we provide a brief overview of this research topic in the literature, followed by an in-depth explanation of the compliant movement primitives framework, with details on both statistical generalization and transition graphs. An extensive experimental evaluation demonstrates the applicability and the usefulness of the approach.

Keywords: compliant movements, adaptive system, learning system, robot control, learning by demonstration

1. Introduction

The need to operate in unstructured environments, such as human everyday environments and homes, drives the development of algorithms for fast generation of new trajectories of robots in compliant behavior mode without sacrificing tracking accuracy. Operating in unstructured environments and with humans requires compliant robot behavior because of possible unplanned contact with objects, and more importantly, with humans themselves. To achieve such behavior, accurate dynamical models of the robot and the task are needed [1].

Yet, acquisition of accurate dynamical models of robots and more specifically of robots performing a task, are difficult to obtain. Therefore, different methods, including biologically inspired methods, were proposed for robot control [2]. Other approaches have been proposed for torque learning. For example, Nguyen-Tuong and Peters [3, 4] relied on local Gaussian process regression (GPR) and used it for on-line dynamic model learning. Their approaches improve the accuracy of the model while avoiding high feedback gains. On the other hand, their method requires the availability of a large quantity of data in order to fully learn a complete dynamic model, and not only task-specific torques. Learning of torques for a specific task can be utilized using iterative learning control (ILC) [5] as was shown in the paper of Schwarz and Behnke [6], who used ILC to learn motor and friction models. Similarly, Gautier et al. [7] proposed an iterative learning identification and control method for dynamic robot control.

The latest generations of robotic mechanisms, such as the Kuka LWR-4, are equipped with joint-torque sensors [8], which can be used to measure the torques during the operation. The possibility of recording joint torques has been exploited in several approaches for learning of task-specific joint torques. One such method is with the use of compliant movement primitives (CMPs), first introduced by Petrič et al. [9] and later adopted by [10, 11], which encode both the kinematic trajectory as well as the corresponding joint torques.

The main topic of this chapter is a review of compliant movement primitives (CMPs), which are suitable for robots with active torque control. CMPs enable accurate execution while maintaining a compliant mode of operation, without requiring explicit models of task dynamics. CMPs draw their inspiration from the human ability to learn arbitrary dynamical tasks [12]. They can be easily learned from user demonstrations. In this paper, we present the basics of the CMPs, followed by the means to surpass the limited applicability of pure imitation through generation of new, previously untrained movements. In order to do so, two mathematical means were exploited: statistical generalization, which allows for variation in task configuration, and hierarchical database search, which allows combinations of previously trained tasks.

Both statistical generalization and hierarchical database search have been previously employed in robotics on a kinematic level. For example, generation of kinematic trajectories with statistical generalization using locally weighted regression was shown in [13]. The method was applied to dynamic movement primitives (DMPs) [14], which also constitute the kinematic part of the CMPs. Similarly, Forte et al. used Gaussian process regression to generalize between the weights of the DMPs [15]. Other approaches of generalization, not relying on DMPs, are thoroughly discussed in [16]. Hierarchical database presented in this chapter consist of transition graphs, that is, motion graphs on each level. It was shown that smooth transitions between movements can be found if they are organized in motion graphs [17]. While Koval et al. [18] used motion graphs to generate different styles of locomotion, Yamane et al. [19, 20] combined them with a binary tree database. Similar work on hierarchical databases was also done by Deniša et al. [11, 21].

Compliant movement primitives are composed of both kinematic and dynamic trajectories. While the first, kinematic part, is encoded as the aforementioned DMPs, the latter, dynamic part, is encoded as a set of radial basis functions. Only the combination of both allows accurate and compliant execution of trajectories. Similar approaches have recently appeared in the literature. An approach that utilizes tactile sensors to determine the force of contact with the environment on the iCub robot, and calculate the joint torques from the measured arm pose was proposed by Calandra et al. [22]. The authors propose using calculated joint-torques in a feed-forward manner for the control, just as is the case in CMPs. Similarly, Steinmetz et al. [23] recorded joint torques along the kinematic trajectory, encoded as a DMP, and used these torques as a feed-forward signal for the controller to increase the accuracy in the next execution of the in-contact task.

The need for robot operations in unstructured environments, combined with the complexity of the acquisition of dynamical models of various tasks, and the occurrence of similar methods in the literature all point at the applicability of the proposed compliant movement primitives approach for robots that go beyond the factory floor.

This chapter is structured as follows. We first provide the details the CMPs, explaining both the kinematic and the dynamic aspects. Generation of new trajectories with statistical generalization and hierarchical database search is explained in Section 3. Experimental evaluation is given in Section 4, followed by a Discussion and a Conclusion.

2. Compliant movement primitives

Compliant movement primitives CMPs are defined as a combination of Dynamic movement primitives (DMPs) for encoding kinematic trajectories and corresponding task-specific dynamics encoded in Torque Primitives (TPs). They are defined as

$$\boldsymbol{h}(t)=\left[\ddot{\boldsymbol{p}}_d(t),\ \dot{\boldsymbol{p}}_d(t),\ \boldsymbol{p}_d(t),\boldsymbol{\tau}_f(t)\right], \tag{1}$$

where $\ddot{\mathbf{p}}_d(t)$, $\dot{\mathbf{p}}_d(t)$, $\mathbf{p}_d(t)$, are the desired acceleration, velocity, and position encoded in the DMPs and $\boldsymbol{\tau}_f(t)$ are the corresponding task-specific dynamics, that is, joint torques or forces, encoded in TPs.

The learning of CMPs is done in three different stages. The first stage is learning the kinematic trajectory for the DMPs. The second stage is learning of corresponding torque or force profiles for TPs, and the last, third, stage is the execution of CMPs. While the learning of kinematic trajectories in the form of DMPs is well documented [13–15, 24], the literature for learning TPs is not as vast [10, 25].

2.1. Control structure

The basic control structure for robot control using CMPs is shown in **Figure 1**. The main advantage of the proposed control architecture is the model free approach which in the execution step enables natural compliant behavior while ensuring sufficient accuracy of the desired movement. Natural compliance is the compliance of the mechanism itself. Because the robot is compliant while executing the task, the forces in case of an unforeseen collision are small. Thus, the robot can perform tasks in unstructured environment and safely interact with humans.

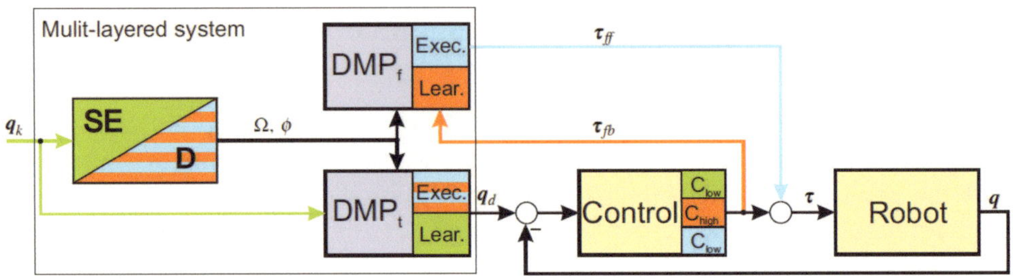

Figure 1. Block diagram of the multi-layered and multi-stage control system. The colored lines (green, orange, and blue) are only active when a chosen state is active (see text for detailed description).

Figure 1 shows the structure of the proposed multi-step control algorithm. The colors indicate which block is active in each step: green—learning of the DMPs, orange—learning of the TPs, and blue—execution of the CMPs. Note that black connections are always active, regardless of the step.

Assuming the robot consists of rigid bodies, the joint space equations of motion can be written in a form

$$\boldsymbol{H}(\boldsymbol{q})\ddot{\boldsymbol{q}}+\boldsymbol{C}(\boldsymbol{q},\dot{\boldsymbol{q}})+\boldsymbol{g}(\boldsymbol{q})+\epsilon(\ddot{\boldsymbol{q}},\dot{\boldsymbol{q}},\boldsymbol{q})=\boldsymbol{\tau}, \tag{2}$$

where $\ddot{\mathbf{q}}, \dot{\mathbf{q}}, \mathbf{q}$ are the joint acceleration, velocity, and position, respectively; $\boldsymbol{H}(\mathbf{q})$ is the inertia matrix, $\mathbf{C}(\mathbf{q}, \dot{\mathbf{q}})$ are the Coriolis and centripetal forces, $\mathbf{g}(\mathbf{q})$ are the gravity forces, and $\epsilon(\ddot{\mathbf{q}}, \dot{\mathbf{q}}, \mathbf{q})$ are additional nonlinearities, for example, friction. We denote the full robot dynamic model as $\mathbf{f}_{robot}(\ddot{\mathbf{q}}, \dot{\mathbf{q}}, \mathbf{q})$. Note that this inverse dynamic model $\mathbf{f}_{robot}(\ddot{\mathbf{q}}, \dot{\mathbf{q}}, \mathbf{q})$ does not include dynamics of the task.

In general, the common approach for tracking the desired motion is using the impedance control given with

$$\boldsymbol{\tau}_u = \boldsymbol{K}\left(\boldsymbol{q}_d - \boldsymbol{q}\right) + \boldsymbol{D}\left(\dot{\boldsymbol{q}}_d - \dot{\boldsymbol{q}}\right) + \boldsymbol{f}_{robot}(\ddot{\boldsymbol{q}},\dot{\boldsymbol{q}},\boldsymbol{q}) + \boldsymbol{\tau}_f, \tag{3}$$

where $\mathbf{K}$ and $\mathbf{D}$ are the diagonal matrices of the desired stiffness and damping respectively [1], $\boldsymbol{q}_d$ is the vector of desired motion encoded in DMPs, and $\boldsymbol{\tau}_f$ is the vector of task-specific torques encoded in TPs. Here, if the values of $\mathbf{K}$ are high, the robot is accurately tracking the trajectory with high error rejection ratio, that is, with stiff behavior. Vice versa, if the values of $\mathbf{K}$ are low, the robot cannot accurately track the desired trajectory unless additional task-specific torques $\boldsymbol{\tau}_f$ are provided.

In the following, we explain the three steps of the CMPs learning approach: (1) learning of DMPs, (2) learning of TPs, C) execution of CMPs with accurate trajectory tracking and compliant behavior.

2.2. Learning of DMPs

The aim of the first step was to learn the task-specific trajectories of motion, encoded in DMPs. There are several possibilities on how to gain and encoded the motion in DMPs for both periodic and point-to-point motions [13–14, 24]. A short recap fallows on how to encode motions based on human demonstrations for point-to-point DMPs. The equations below are valid for one DOF and can be used in parallel for multiple DOFs. A DMPs is defined as a nonlinear system of differential equations

$$v\dot{z} = \alpha_z\left(\beta_z\left(g - y\right) - z\right) + f\left(s\right), \tag{4}$$

$$v\dot{y} = z. \tag{5}$$

Here, the linear part ensures that y converges to the desired goal configuration once $f(s)$ becomes zero. $f(s)$ is a nonlinear part that defines the shape of the movement. It is given by

$$f\left(s\right) = \frac{\Sigma_{b=1}^{L_d} w_{qb}\Psi_b\left(s\right)}{\Sigma_{b=1}^{L_d}\Psi_b\left(s\right)}. \tag{6}$$

Here, the Gaussian basis functions $\psi_b(s)$ are defined as

$$\psi_b\left(s\right) = exp\left(-d_b\left(s - c_b\right)^2\right), \tag{7}$$

where c_b are centers and d_b are widths of the Gaussians. Since $f(s)$ is not directly time dependent, the phase variable s was introduced as

$$v\dot{s} = -\alpha_s s. \tag{8}$$

The phase variable is common across all DMPs and TPs, for example, it is common for all CMPs. With proper selection of parameters α_z, β_z, α_s and v, the convergence of the system is guaranteed. For evaluation, the parameters were set empirically to $\alpha_y = 48$, $\beta_z = \alpha_z/4$ and $\alpha_s = 2$.

To acquire weights w_{qb} that represent the desired motion, the target for learning is derived from Eqs. (4) and (5). It is given by

$$f_{target} = v^2\ddot{q}_{xn}(t_i) + \alpha_z\dot{q}_{xn}(t_i) - \alpha_z\beta_z(g - q_{xn}(t_i)), i = 1,\ldots,T, \quad (9)$$

where the goal g is defined by the end value of the example trajectory $q_{xn}(t_T)$. To calculate weights w_{qb}, the overdetermined system (Eq. (9)) is solved using regression technic for each joint. Note that recursive regression [26] is also possible, which is a common choice for online imitation learning.

2.3. Learning of TPs

Once DMPs are learned, learning of TPs follows. This step is denoted with orange color in the block scheme given in **Figure 1**. Here, we give a short recap of the method that exploits stiff and accurate robot behavior in a supervised environment.

The TPs are given as a combination of Gaussian functions denoted by

$$\tau_f = \frac{\sum_{b=1}^{L_d} w_{tb}\psi_b(s)}{\sum_{b=1}^{L_d}\psi_b(s)}. \quad (10)$$

To gain corresponding torques for accurate tracking of the trajectory, the gain $\boldsymbol{K}$ is set to "high." Note that this usually implies stiff robot behavior; therefore, the action must be performed under human supervision. To acquire weights w_{tb} that represent the corresponding torques, the target for learning is given in a form of

$$f_{TP-target} = K(q_d - q) + D(\dot{q}_d - \dot{q}). \quad (11)$$

where y is the desired motion trajectory encoded in DMPs (Eqs. (4) and (5)). Using the same approach as in DMPs, the weights w_{tb} from Eq. (10) are calculated using a recursive regression [26] for each joint. The details on learning TPs are in [10].

2.4. Execution of CMPs

Once both, the DMPs and TPs are learned, the CMPs can be executed using the control law given by Eq. (3). This step is denoted with blue color in the block scheme given in **Figure 1**. Because the task-specific dynamics is provided in a feed-forward manner, the tracking accuracy remains high even if the feedback gains are much lower that during learning. By selecting lower feedback gains, it is assumed that the robot behavior is compliant. However, since feedback gains are low and the robot behavior is complaint, the error rejection ratio is small, from which follows that the tracking is only accurate as long as the system is not heavily perturbed.

Note that the main idea of the CMPs is that the feed-forward part assures the nominal behavior of the robot for a specific given task even in cases when low feedback gains are used. In this way, good tracking and compliant behavior are achieved at the same time.

3. Autonomous generation of CMPs

Learning CMPs by human demonstration greatly simplifies execution of tasks in a compliant manner, as it does not need mathematically defined dynamic models in advance. But doing this for each variation of a dynamically versatile task is unpractical and time-consuming. In the following, two example expansions of the initial CMP database are presented to overcome this issue. While the first subsection tackles the issue of generating completely CMPs using a search in hierarchical databases with transition graphs, the second delivers the methodology for using statistical techniques in order to generalize CMPs.

3.1. Hierarchical database search

This section presents combining available trajectories to generate new trajectories with the corresponding feed-forward torque control signals using hierarchical graph search. Generating new robot movements through hierarchical graph search as such is not new, see for example, [20, 21]. To apply the hierarchical graph search on CMPs, the database of CMPs needs to be divided into two parts: the primary part that includes the kinematic trajectories and the secondary one that includes the dynamic part of CMPs, that is, corresponding torques. As new kinematic trajectories are synthesized through hierarchical search in the initial database, corresponding torques are extracted from the secondary part of the database.

3.1.1. Building the database

The primary part of the database, which stores kinematic part of CMPs, that is, position trajectories $\boldsymbol{q}_d$, is a binary tree-like structure with transition graphs at each level. As the primary database is built, the secondary part is added. It encodes the dynamic part of CMPs, that is, corresponding torques $\boldsymbol{\tau}_f$. Database construction begins with concatenating initial example position trajectories into a sample position matrix

$$\boldsymbol{X} = [\boldsymbol{x}_1, \boldsymbol{x}_2, \ldots, \boldsymbol{x}_F], \tag{12}$$

where $\boldsymbol{x}_i$ denotes a state vector sampled at a given discrete time interval, and F the total number of all samples belonging to all example trajectories included in the database. A state vector, defined as

$$\boldsymbol{x}_i = [q_{x1}, \dot{q}_{x1}, q_{x2}, \dot{q}_{x2}, \ldots, q_{xP}, \dot{q}_{xP}], \tag{13}$$

where subscript x denotes examples, and P number of DOF represents positions and velocities of an example trajectory at a given discrete time interval.

The sample motion matrix, encapsulating all example potion trajectories, represents a root node of a binary tree. See **Figure 2** for a simple representation of the database. A k-means algorithm, with $k = 2$, is used to cluster similar state vectors and split the initial root node into two child nodes. Clustering is then used again on each of the two child nodes, and thus, the nodes at the next level are gained. This can also be seen in **Figure 2** depicting a simple example of a database. The nodes keep splitting until the criterion, based on the variability of the data in node, is met. The mean distance d_k of a node k, used as a "stop split" criterion, is defined as

$$d_k = \frac{\Sigma_{i=1}^{n_k} d\left(\boldsymbol{x}_{ki}, \boldsymbol{c}_k\right)}{n_k}, \tag{14}$$

where n_k denotes the number of state vectors clustered in node k. Euclidian distance $d(\boldsymbol{x}_{ki}, \boldsymbol{c}_k)$ is calculated between each state vector in the node and the node's centroid $\boldsymbol{c}_k$, gained by the k-means algorithm. As this criterion indicates the similarity of the clustered state vectors, the database does not get unnecessary deep, while the precision of the representation remains satisfactory. The clustering is continued until all nodes meet the "stop split" criterion. Every branch is extended as a leaf node until the last layer. In this way, all the state vectors are represented at all the database levels.

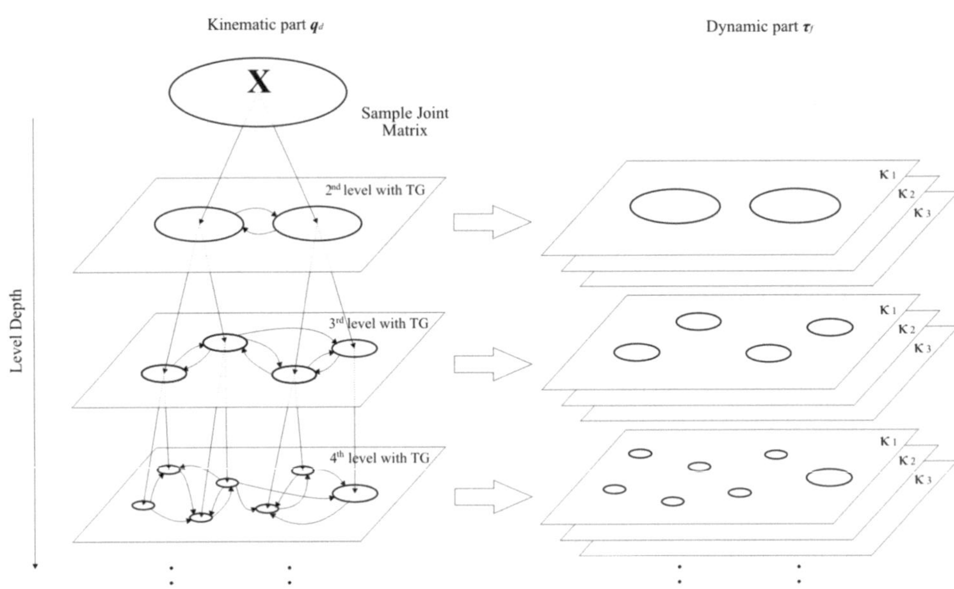

Figure 2. A simple representation of used database. The primary part encoding kinematic trajectories and with transition graphs is shown on the left. The secondary part which encapsulates corresponding torques and has multiple layers per level is depicted on the right side.

Every level of the database includes a transition graph representing all possible transitions between the nodes (see **Figure 2**). The graph's edge weights define the probability of transition from one node to the other. The transition probability from node k to node l is estimated by

$$P_{kl} = \frac{m_{kl}}{n_k} \tag{15}$$

where m_{kl} denotes the number of all state vectors clustered in node k that have a successor in node l, that is, the number of transitions observed in all trajectories of the original data. As state vectors are not needed any more, they are omitted, and at each node, a mean of corresponding state vectors $\bar{\mathbf{x}}_k$ is saved instead. At this point, the time component is also lost, which is tackled later on in this section.

While the already constructed primary part of database encodes CMP's kinematic trajectories, the secondary part will encode the dynamic part. The torques signals are not separately clustered, but rather associated with corresponding nodes in the primary database. For each part of the kinematic trajectories, represented in a single node through the mean of state vectors, a corresponding mean of the torques signal $\bar{\tau}_f$ and its time durations is stored. As the same kinematic movement can have different dynamic parts, this is done multiple times for each dynamic task descriptor. See **Figure 2** for example representation of the whole database.

3.1.2. *Synthesizing new CMPs*

A new trajectory is defined by first selecting the desired start and end points on two different trajectories. A dynamic task descriptor, for example, the desired task time multiplier k, is also selected. As the level determines, the fidelity of reproduction compared to the original trajectories, the last level of the hierarchical database is usually selected. A path between the nodes corresponding to the desired start and end joint position needs to be found. To achieve that A* search algorithm, it is used on the transition graph at the desired level. As long as the two trajectories share a similar enough part, the most probable path is found and with it a sequence of nodes, that is, mean state vectors.

Based on the selected dynamic task descriptor, for example, k, we add the corresponding mean torques $\bar{\boldsymbol{\tau}}_f$ to the state vectors $\bar{\mathbf{x}}_k$ of the discovered sequence. We enhance this sequence further with time durations t_d corresponding to the added torques. A sequence of positions, torques, and their time durations is gained. The newly discovered sequence can be written as

$$\left\{ (\bar{x}_1, \tau_{f1}, 0), \left(\bar{x}_2, \tau_{f2}, \frac{t_{d1} + t_{d2}}{2} \right), \dots, \left(\bar{x}_r, \tau_{fr}, \frac{t_{d(r-1)} + t_{dr}}{2} \right) \right\}, \tag{16}$$

where r denotes the number of nodes on the trajectory.

A trajectory from each discovered sequence is generated by encoding it as a DMP. The DMPs describing newly synthesized kinematic trajectories and the corresponding torque control signals (encoded as TPs) can then be used to execute new, not directly shown, movements while remaining compliant.

3.2. Statistical generalization

Using programming by demonstration approaches to learn CMPs can simplify compliant execution of dynamically versatile tasks. But executing demonstrations for each possible variation of the task would be time-consuming and cumbersome. For each new task descriptor, a new CMP needs to be learned, that is, motion trajectory needs to be learned through human demonstrations and executed on a robot for torque learning. Even if the deviation happens just on the torque level, for example, because of different payload, supervised learning of the torque is needed. Besides using actions graphs to generate new CMPs, as seen in the previous section, statistical generalization techniques can be employed. For that, a set of learned CMPs which transition smoothly between each other as a function of task descriptors, that is, query points, is needed. Using generalization, a task can be executed at an arbitrary query point $\boldsymbol{c}$ within the learned query space.

For statistical generalization, we use Gaussian process regression (GPR), which can be used to learn a function

$$F : c \mapsto [w_q, g_q, w_\tau, v] \tag{17}$$

A CMP, defined by w_q, g_q, w_τ, and v, can be used to execute a task, defined by a query c, in a compliant manner. By the above definition, F computes appropriate CMP parameters at the given query c, that is, at a given task variation.

Once the Gaussian process is *trained* using example training sets of CMPs, new appropriate CMPs for given queries c can be calculated by simple matrix multiplications, which can easily be accomplished in real time.

4. Evaluation

To evaluate the CMPs, a robotic arm with a mounted hand was used. The Kuka LWR-IV anthropomorphic arm was used. It has seven degrees of freedom and, important for the presented approach, torque sensors at each joint. We omit further details, for example, internal parameters, of the robotic arm and refer the reader to [8]. In order to grasp objects, a three fingered BarrettHand BH8-280 was mounted at the end of the robotic arm. Further details on grasping are omitted, as this is not the focus of the chapter. While the approach based on the CMPs does not need the dynamical model of the robot, the dynamical model of the Kuka robot was used in all experiments. Note that the controller for the Kuka robot does not allow to fully disengage the dynamical model. However, using the CMPs, any possible model errors are compensated.

Evaluation of CMPs first focuses on estimating the quality of tracking the desired trajectory under various stiffness settings by measuring the errors between desired and actual robot trajectory. Here, the CMP approach was compared to a standard high-gain feedback control approach. Next the behavior of both systems when colliding with an unforeseen object was evaluated. The last part is concerned with evaluation of autonomously generated CMPs using the statistical graph search and evaluation of generalized CMPs.

4.1. Tracking accuracy evaluation

The analysis of tracking was performed on a pick-and-place task. The performance of the approach based on CMPs was compared with a common feedback approach. The evaluation setup can be seen in **Figure 6**, where a snapshot shows an example of pick-and-place movement. The initial movement trajectory for pick and place was demonstrated using kinesthetic guidance and encoded in DMPs as a part of CMPs. As the DMPs have been studied previously, we omit their specific evaluation and refer the reader to [13, 14, 24]. The demonstrated trajectory was then executed several times, using stiff robot control, that is, high feedback gains, which ensure accurate trajectory tracking. While executing the motion, the corresponding torques were obtained and encoded as CMPs. For evaluation, the mass of the object that the robot was holding was changed from 0.5 kg up to 4.5 kg with a step of 1 kg.

The movement was then executed using the complete CMPs, that is, including feed-forward torques, under different feedback gain settings. For comparison, for each object mass, several executions were performed by varying feedback gain parameters without using feed-forward torques, that is, using a common stiffens controller. To identify the tracking accuracy of the controllers, the maximum tracking error for each task execution was calculated. The maximal tracking error is defined as

$$e_m = \max_t (\| \boldsymbol{p}_a(t) - \boldsymbol{p}_d(t) \|), \tag{18}$$

Where $\mathbf{p_a}(t)$ is the current robot position on the trajectory, and the $\mathbf{p}_d(t)$ is the desired position of the trajectory, both in Cartesian space. The task was performed for several different feedback gains settings going from 50 Nm/rad up to 2000 Nm/rad, selected so that covered a wide spectrum of compliance exhibited by a Kuka LWR-IV robot.

Results of the evaluation are shown in **Figure 3**, where we can see the mean and standard deviation of the e_m over all feedback gain settings and for each object weights. We can clearly see here that the tracking accuracy is much larger if only feedback control is used compared to the novel approach based on CMPs. The plot also shows the point where the tracking error starts to increase notably, regardless of the approach, which was 50 Nm/rad. Based on this results, the feedback gains for future evaluation were set to $K = 50$ Nm/rad.

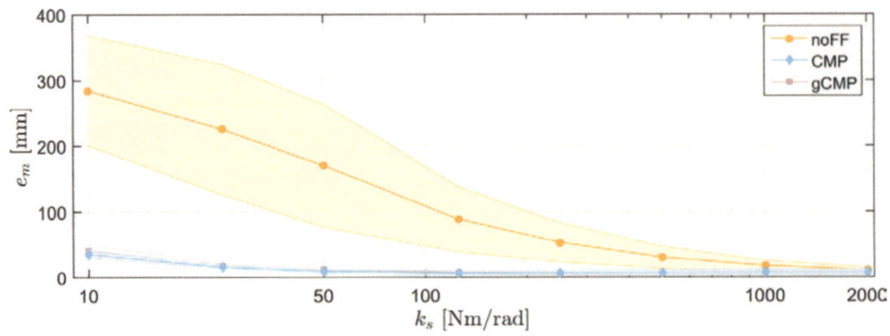

Figure 3. Mean and standard deviation of task's maximum error for different the object masses. The CMP indicates the performance CMPs system, while the noFF indicates the mean and standard deviation for the feedback control without feed-forward torque signal. The gCMP indicates the performance of the generalized CMPs trajectories.

4.2. Contact evaluation

To evaluate the behavior of CMP-based control approach, while colliding with an unforeseen object, or an environment, a downward motion was demonstrated first, and then executed to train the CMP. During learning the movement was executed in a free space, without any contacts. To evaluate the forces and behavior when robot collides with an unforeseen object or environment, an object was placed in the path of the robot. The behavior of the robot when colliding was analyzed for three different cases: impedance control with high gains ($K = 2000$ Nm/rad), impedance control with low gains ($K = 50$ Nm/rad), and previously learned CMP with ($K = 50$ Nm/rad).

The results of impact are shown in **Figure 4**, where we can see that in case of high feedback gains the tracking error remains relatively small thorough the movement. However, in this

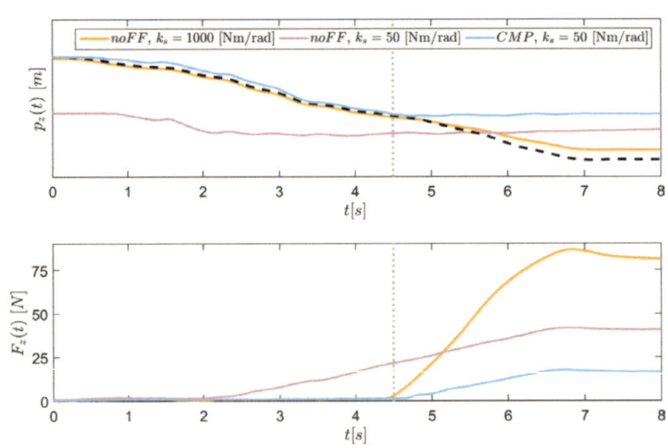

Figure 4. Robot colliding with an object while using different stiffness settings and control approaches. The graphs present collision trajectories and forces under two different stiffness settings ($K = 1000$ Nm/rad and $K = 50$ Nm/rad) and with two different control approaches (noFF and CMP). The top plot shows the actual robot task space position in vertical (z) axis, and the bottom plot shows TCP forces in the vertical (z) axis.

http://dx.doi.org/10.5772/64058

case, the forces rise significantly when the robot is in the contact with the environment. Vice versa, if the robot is compliant, that is, if the feedback gains are low, the forces are small, but the tracking accuracy is poor. Finally, CMPs combine both positive aspects: good tracking accuracy before contact and low interaction forces once the contact is established.

4.3. Hierarchical graph evaluation

Hierarchical graph approach was also evaluated using a Kuka LWR-IV robot arm. The demonstrator taught the robot several reaching movements while kinesthetically guiding the arm. Two examples of the learned movements that intersect each were shown. DMPs were used to encode all kinematic trajectories. They were used in the second step to obtain corresponding torque control signals, as described previously. Each movement was executed three times with different task time multipliers $\kappa = \{1,2,3\}$. The learned movement trajectories q_d and the corresponding torque control signals τ_f were used to execute the learned reaching CMP using a low-gain feedback controller.

As described in Section 3.1, the database was built using learned CMPs and used to find new reaching movements. A* search algorithm found new sequences of nodes, as the demonstrated trajectories had parts that were sufficiently similar. Each new sequence started in the first node of one of the demonstrated trajectories and ended in the final node of one of the others. Each new sequence of mean position was then enhanced with mean torques and corresponding time duration three times, once per task time multiplier. Using DMPs, a complete representation of new reaching movement's trajectories was synthesized. A close-up of transitions of two example demonstrated and newly synthesized movements is shown in **Figure 5**. Smooth and continuous transitions can be observed. In order to evaluate transitions of corresponding torque signals, tracking error was observed during executions of example demonstrated CMPs and newly generated CMPs. No significant rise in errors could be observed.

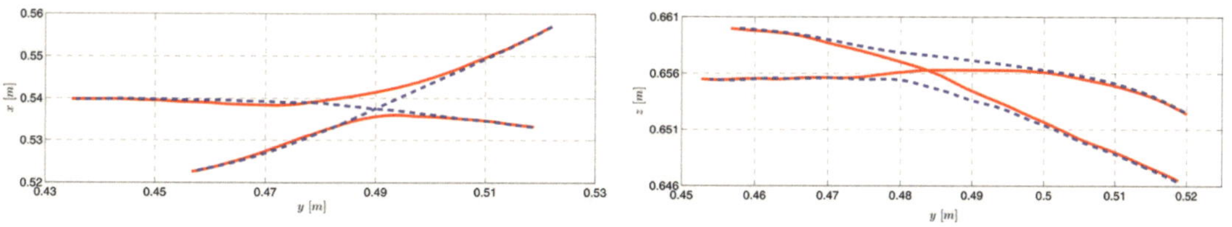

Figure 5. Smooth and continuous transition can be observed in a close-up of two example demonstrated and newly synthesized movements. Original demonstrated movements are denoted by red color, while newly synthesized are marked with a dashed blue line.

4.4. Statistical generalization evaluation

Evaluation of statistical generalization can be done by comparing generalized CMPs to learned non-generalized CMPs. The selected task was a pick-and place task. Evaluation setup can be seen in **Figure 6**. A trajectory $\mathbf{q}_S(\mathbf{t})$, which successfully moves a hand weight from the initial position to the final position, was demonstrated by kinesthetic guidance. It was then executed five times using a standard high-gain controller which ensures high tracking accuracy. Mass of the object was changed each time. In this way, five different CMPs were learned, each having the same kinematic component and a different dynamic one. This set was used with statistical generalization techniques in order to generalize them over a one dimensional query, that is, a varying object mass. Generalized CMPs could compliantly move an object with arbitrary mass within the training space. New, generalized, CMPs were executed for nine different queries, covering demonstrated weights as well as points in between. Tracking errors were recorded for each execution. Each new generalized CMP was executed at eight different stiffness settings. Tracking errors were recorded for each execution. By comparing the maximum tracking errors of generalized CMPs to maximum tracking errors gained by executing learned CMPs, a slight but not statistically significant, increase in tracking error was observed. The errors prevailed at lower stiffness settings as the system is more susceptible to inaccuracies in generalized torque signals.

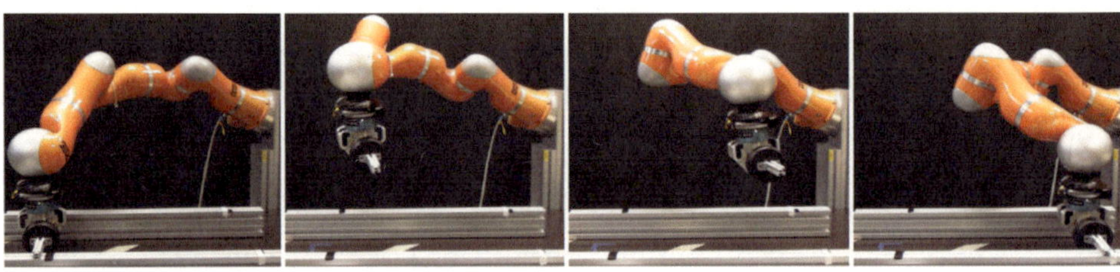

Figure 6. Experimental set-up for statistical generalization evaluation. The robot executed a pick-and-place task. Each execution the object weight was varied.

5. Discussion

In order to be efficient, robots need to autonomously react to the changes of the external conditions, such as changes in the environment or in the task. Relying on pure reproduction of learned motion will not provide the robots sufficient possibilities to reach to different situations, as learning to cover for all situations is simply impossible—the number of possibilities is far too great.

In this aspect, both presented methods of autonomous CMP generation, either through a hierarchical database search or through statistical generalization, expand the realm of learned motions to new, previously unexplored solutions. While the first method combines parts of demonstrated trajectories, the second one generates completely new trajectories within the database of learned motions. These new trajectories resemble the previously learned ones, that is, they have similar properties. The challenge of generating completely new motions using CMPs remains an open issue. While explorative methods, such as reinforcement learning methods, could be used to learn completely new motions with respect to a given reward, such methods are also known for requiring a large number of iterations. These might make practical use less convenient.

As an alternative to CMPs, dynamical models could be used. Here, it is important to note that CMPs model the complete task, for example, the task of interaction with a deformable object. Obtaining a dynamical model of a robot might be feasible, specifically for an expert, but obtaining a dynamical model for numerous tasks, such as the aforementioned task of interaction with a deformable object, might be extremely difficult, if not impossible. Thus, CMPs offer the means to solve this problem, as modeling is not needed, but they tend to solve it for one task at a time. Again, the presented methods of adapting to the changes of the task allow for learning of complete families of tasks from a small set of demonstrations.

Obtaining the CMPs is another area which requires further research, as currently these are obtained in a supervised manner during stiff robot behavior. Thus, the effort for the user still remains considerable. While we have proposed initial solutions in autonomously obtaining torque profiles in [25], a general method still remains an open research issue.

In conclusion, we have presented the CMP framework and two methods that expand the realm of possible application beyond simple imitation. The CMP framework, which bypasses the need for accurate dynamical modeling, was extensively evaluated and has been shown to offer a viable opportunity for compliant and at the same time accurate robotic behavior.

Acknowledgements

The research leading to these results has been partially founded from the European Community's Seventh Framework Programme FP7/2007-2013 (Specific Programme Cooperation, Theme 3, Information and Communication Technologies) under Grant agreement no. 600578, ACAT.

Author details

Miha Deniša*, Tadej Petrič, Andrej Gams and Aleš Ude

*Address all correspondence to: miha.denisa@ijs.si

Department of Automatics, Biocybernetics and Robotics, Jožef Stefan Institute, Ljubljana, Slovenija

References

[1] Albu-Schaffer A., Eiberger O., Grebenstein M., Haddadin S., Ott C., Wimbock T., Wolf S., and Hirzinger G. Soft robotics. IEEE Robotics and Automation Magazine. 2008;15(3):20–30.

[2] Franklin D.W., and Wolpert D.M. Computational mechanisms of sensorimotor control. Neuron. 2011;72(3):425–442.

[3] Nguyen-Tuong D., and Peters J. Learning robot dynamics for computed torque control using local Gaussian processes regression. In: ECSIS symposium learning and adaptive behaviors for robotic systems; Edinburgh, Scotland, UK. 2008. p. 59–64.

[4] Nguyen-Tuong D., and Peters J. Model learning for robot control: a survey. Cognitive Processing. 2011;12(4):319–340.

[5] Bristow D.A., Tharayil M., and Alleyne A.G. A survey of iterative learning control. IEEE Control Systems. 2006;26(3):96–114.

[6] Schwarz M., and Behnke S. Compliant robot behavior using servo actuator models identified by iterative learning control. In: Proceedings of 17th robo cup international symposium; Eindhoven, Netherlands. 2013. p. 207–218.

[7] Gautier M., Jubien A., and Janot A. Iterative learning identification and computed torque control of robots. In: IEEE/RSJ international conference on intelligent robots and systems (IROS); Tokyo, Japan. 2013. p. 3419–3424.

[8] Bischoff R., Kurth J., Schreiber G., Koeppe R., Albu-Schaeffer A., Beyer A., Eiberger O., Haddadin S., Stemmer A., Grunwald G., and Hirzinger G. The KUKA-DLR Lightweight Robot arm—a new reference platform for robotics research and manufacturing. In: 41st international symposium on robotics; 2010.

[9] Petrič T., Gams A., Žlajpah L., and Ude A. Online learning of task-specific dynamics for periodic tasks. In: Intelligent robots and systems (IROS 2014); Chicago, IL, USA. 2014. p. 1790–1795.

[10] Deniša M., Gams A., Ude A., and Petrič T. Learning compliant movement primitives through demonstration and statistical generalization. IEEE/ASME Transactions on Mechatronics. 2015; (99):1.

[11] Deniša M., Petrič T., Asfour T., and Ude A. Synthesizing compliant reaching movements by searching a database of example trajectories. In: International conference on humanoid robots; Atlanta, GA, USA. 2013. p. 540–546.

[12] Krakauer J. W., Ghilardi M.F., and Ghez C. Independent learning of internal models for kinematic and dynamic control of reaching. Nature Neuroscience. 1999;2(11):1026–1031.

[13] Ude A., Gams A., Asfour T., and Morimoto J. Task-specific generalization o discrete and periodic dynamic movement primitives. IEEE Transactions on Robotics.2010;26(5): 800–815.

[14] Ijspeert A.J., Nakanishi J., Hoffmann H., Pastor P., and Schaal S. Dynamical movement primitives: learning attractor models for motor behaviors. Neural Computing. 2013;25(2):328–373.

[15] Forte D., Gams A., Morimoto J., and Ude A. On-line motion synthesis and adaptation using a trajectory database. Robotics and Autonomous Systems. 2012;60(10):1327–1339.

[16] Calinon S. A tutorial on task-parameterized movement learning and retrieval. Intelligent Service Robotics. 2015;9(1):1–29.

[17] Rose C., Cohen M.F., and Bodenheimer B. Verbs and adverbs: multidimensional motion interpolation. IEEE Computer Graphics and Applications. 1998;18(5):32–40.

[18] Kovar L., Gleicher M., and Pighin F. Motion Graphs. ACM Transactions on Graphics. 2002;21(3):473–482

[19] Yamane K., Revfi M., and Asfour T. Synthesizing object receiving motions of humanoid robots with human motion database. In: IEEE international conference on robotics and automation (ICRA); Karlsruhe, Germany. 2013. p. 1621–1628.

[20] Yamane K., Yamaguchi Y., and Nakamura Y. Human motion database with a binary tree and node transition graphs. Autonomous Robots. 2010;30(1):87–98.

[21] Deniša M., and Ude A. Synthesis of new dynamic movement primitives through search in a hierarchical database of example movements. Int J Adv Robot Syst. 2015;12(137): 1–13

[22] Calandra R., Ivaldi S., Deisenroth M., and Peters J. Learning torque control in presence of contacts using tactile sensing from robot skin. In: IEEE-RAS 15th international conference on humanoid robots (Humanoids); Madrid, Spain. 2015. p. 690–695.

[23] Steinmetz F., Montebelli A., and Kyrki V. Simultaneous kinesthetic teaching of positional and force requirements for sequential in-contact tasks. In: IEEE-RAS 15th international conference on humanoid robots (Humanoids); Madrid, Spain. 2015. p. 202–209.

[24] Schaal S., Mohajerian P., and A. Ijspeert A. Dynamics systems vs. optimal control—a unifying view. Progress in Brain Research. 2007;165:425–445.

[25] Petrič T., Colasanto L., Gams A., Ude A., and Ijspeert A.J. Bio-inspired learning and database expansion of compliant movement primitives. In: Humanoid robots (Humanoids); Seoul, Korea. p. 356–351.

[26] Gams A., Ijspeert A.J., Schaal S., and Lenarčič J. On-line learning and modulation of periodic movements with nonlinear dynamical systems. Autonomous Robots. 2009;27(1):3–23.

Chapter 2

Induced Force Hovering of Spherical Robot by Under-Actuated Control of Dual Rotor

G. Santos-Medina, K.Y. Heras-Gaytán,
E.A. Martínez-García, R. Torres-Córdoba and
V. Carrillo-Saucedo

Additional information is available at the end of the chapter

http://dx.doi.org/10.5772/63548

Abstract

This chapter discusses the design and modelling of a spherical flying robot. The main objective is to control its hovering and omnidirectional mobility by controlling the air mass differential pressure between two asynchronous coaxial rotors that are aligned collinearly. The spherical robot design has embedded a gyroscopic mechanism of three rings that allow the rotors' under-actuated mobility with 3DOF. The main objective of this study is to maintain the thrust force with nearly vertical direction. The change in pressure between rotors allows to vary the rotors' tilt and pitch. The system uses special design propellers to improve the laminar air mass flux. A nonlinear fitting model automatically calibrates the rotors' angular speed as a function of digital values. This model is the functional form that represents the reference input to control the rotors' speed, validated by three types controllers: P, PI, and PID. The robot's thrust and induced forces and flight mechanics are proposed and analysed. The simulation results show the feasibility of the approach.

Keywords: flight mechanics, flying control, robot modelling, thrust force, UAV, under-actuation

1. Introduction

Nowadays, unmanned aerial vehicle (UAV) robots are being deployed at an increased rate for numerous applications falling into a variety of engineering fields. There exist numerous kinds of rotary-wing-based robotic technologies in particular with active devices. Robots with rotating wings are capable to self-control over lift, propulsion, landing, hovering And take-off tasks [1–4]. Overcoming vertical flight (with minimum energy cost) is fundamental to accomplish autonomous precise tasks. One fundamental aspect in controlling and designing rotary-wing-based intelligent machines is to consider under-actuated issues to reduce the number of actuators. Under-actuated flying robots perform motion tasks more naturally, taking advantage of the inertial and gravitational forces, consequently, reducing the use of electrical energy. Biological flying birds are instances of extremely efficient under-actuated bodies. Therefore, in order to design flying machines with a reduced number of actuators, it is essential to model and understand the mechanical nature of the robot mechanics, the fluids and their physics-based relationship.

The present work has foundations on the prototype of a home-made spherical aerial robot. Some experiments can be viewed at https://www.youtube.com/watch?v=rrGH1Oh_beM. Nevertheless, the purpose of this chapter is not on showing and discussing experimental results, but on mathematically sustaining the hypothesis of the robot's flight mechanics and control. Unlike, known spherical design approaches [5–7], rather than deploying aileron-like propellers, we proposed yaw, pitch and roll changes through under-actuation exerting an inner gyroscopic mechanism. In the present chapter, the authors are particularly interested in disclosing the physical model of a dual rotary-wing spherical robot with an under-actuated gyroscopic mechanism. The model has been divided into four major areas: the robot's flight mechanics with direct and inverse solution, the thrusting or induced force model, the rotors control model and a proportional integral derivative (PID) based control with non-stationary reference values.

This chapter is organised as follows. In Section 2, the design and mechanical aspects of the aerial robot are presented. Section 3 presents the kinematic direct and inverse solutions of the flight mechanics. In Section 4, the acceleration components and forces involved in the robot's aerodynamics are discussed. Section 5 presents the robot's thrusting force model that involves two collinear induced forces. Section 6 presents the rotors' actuator speed models that are proposed from empirical measurements, and subsequently, the analytical solution is obtained. In Section 7, the actuators' feedback linear control is described. Finally, in Section 8, conclusions are drawn.

2. Spherical gyroscopic robot

Unlike other reported approaches [8–13], in this study, the authors have proposed an omnidirectional spherical design with two rotors vertically collinear (see **Figure 1**, right, and **Figure 2**).

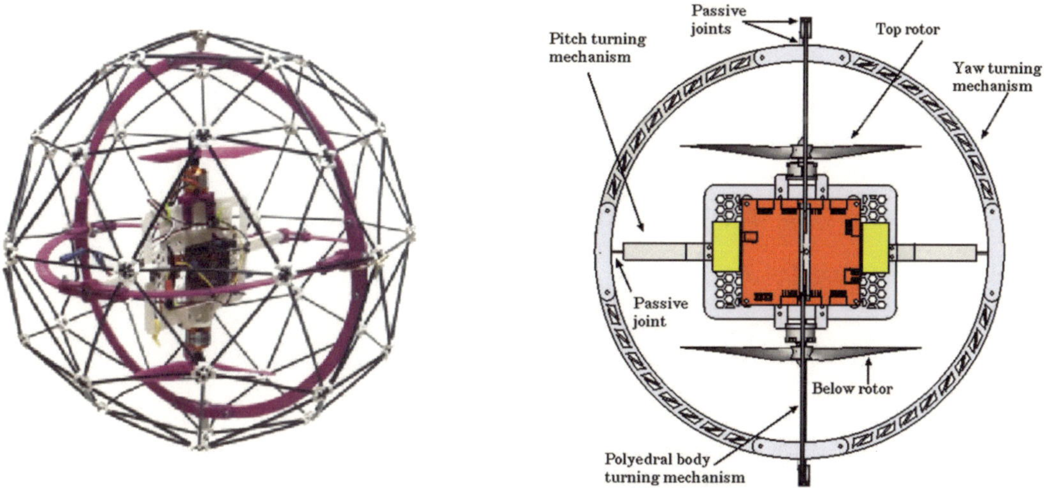

Figure 1. Left: Aerial robot real prototype. Right: Robot's main actuated and under-actuated mechanical elements.

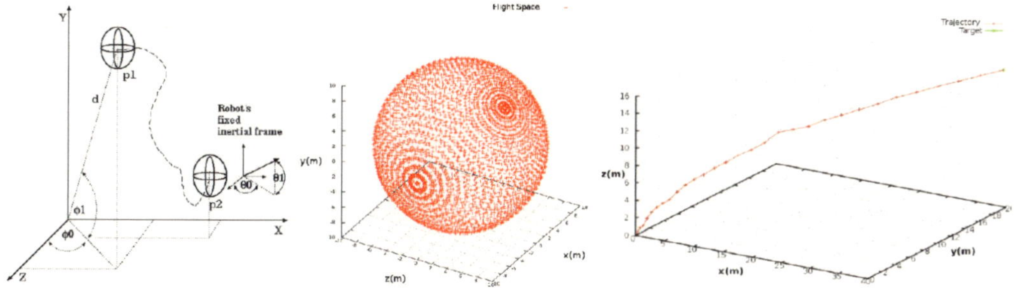

Figure 2. Left: Robot's global and local spherical coordinates. Centre: Robot's flying space (Eqs. (1)–(3)). Right: recursive trajectory generation (Texto) and (Texto).

3. Flight mechanics model

Flight mechanics refers to the study of geometry of flight of a heavier-than-air aircraft, considering aerodynamic aspects. Expressions (1)–(3) model the three-dimension robot's Cartesian kinematic components that describe its motion. The components, namely, x, y and z, are the space positions w.r.t. the location of the robot's starting flight. The proposed kinematic model is constrained with initial posture as the inertial frame origin, where d is the distance between the robot's instantaneous 3D position and its Cartesian origin. Azimuth angle ϕ_0 is w.r.t. the plane XY, and the elevation angle ϕ_1 is w.r.t. the Y-axis:

$$x = d\cos(\phi_1)\sin(\phi_0) \tag{1}$$

The y component (vertical) is expressed as

$$y = d\sin(\phi_1) \tag{2}$$

And, the z component is expressed as

$$z = d\cos(\phi_1)\cos(\phi_0) \tag{3}$$

For further purpose, the inverse solution is obtained by an algebraic arrangement of derivatives. The first-order derivatives of Eqs. (1)–(3) are obtained and shown in Eqs.(4)–(6),

$$\dot{x} = \dot{d}\cos(\phi_1)\sin(\phi_0) + d\cos(\phi_1)\cos(\phi_0)\dot{\phi}_0 - d\sin(\phi_1)\sin(\phi_0)\dot{\phi}_1 \tag{4}$$

The vertical component is expressed as

$$\dot{y} = \dot{d}\sin(\phi_1) + d\cos(\phi_1)\dot{\varphi}_1 \tag{5}$$

And, the z component is expressed as

$$\dot{z} = \dot{d}\cos(\phi_1)\cos(\phi_0) + d\cos(\phi_1)\cos(\phi_0)\dot{\phi}_0 \tag{6}$$

Figure 2 centre depicts the robot's flying space, which is spherical with the Cartesian origin at robot's starting flying task.

Expressing in the matrix form, the first-order derivative $d\mathbf{p}/dt$ w.r.t. time is

$$\dot{p} = \begin{pmatrix} \dot{x} \\ \dot{y} \\ \dot{z} \end{pmatrix} = \begin{pmatrix} dC_1C_0 & -dS_1S_0 & C_1S_0 \\ 0 & dC_1 & S_1 \\ -dC_1C_0 & -dS_1C_0 & C_1C_0 \end{pmatrix} \cdot \begin{pmatrix} \dot{\phi}_0 \\ \dot{\phi}_1 \\ \dot{d} \end{pmatrix} \tag{7}$$

By simplifying, the linear equation of direct kinematic is denoted by the Jacobian matrix **J** and the first-order vector of independent variables,

$$\dot{p} = J\dot{\Phi} \tag{8}$$

In order to obtain a recursive functional form equivalent to previous state variables, the derivatives are expressed in the following manner:

$$\frac{d}{dt}p = J\frac{d}{dt}\Phi \tag{9}$$

Time differentials are eliminated, and the integration operators complete the remaining differentials dp and $d\phi$:

$$\int_{\dot{p}_1}^{\dot{p}_2} dp = J\int_{\dot{\phi}_1}^{\dot{\phi}_2} d\Phi \tag{10}$$

Thus, to solve for the robot's Cartesian position a recursive form is obtained by algebraically reordering. Next, robot's position $\mathbf{p}_{t+1}$ is obtained by successive approximations of ϕ_t until ϕ_f:

$$p_{t+1} = p_t + J\left(\phi_f - \phi_t\right) \tag{11}$$

In addition, the kinematic inverse solution requires the inverse-squared Jacobian matrix, assuming that it is an invertible and non-singular matrix, with non-zero determinant:

$$J^{-1} = \frac{1}{d^2C_1\left(\left[C_1C_0\right]^2 + \left[S_0S_1\right]\right)}\begin{pmatrix} dC_0 & 0 & -dS_0 \\ dC_1S_0S_1 & dC_1^2 & -dC_1C_0S_1 \\ (dC_1)^2 S_0 & -dC_1C_0S_1 & (dC_1)^2 C_0 \end{pmatrix} \tag{12}$$

Therefore, the first-order inverse kinematic is obtained by an algebraic approach:

$$\dot{\Phi} = J^{-1}\dot{p} \tag{13}$$

As described earlier, we complete the differentials dp and $d\phi$:

$$\int_{\dot{\Phi}_1}^{\dot{\Phi}_2} d\Phi = J^{-1}\int_{\dot{p}_1}^{\dot{p}_2} dp \tag{14}$$

By integrating both sides of the equality, respectively, a recursive inverse solution in terms of the rotor's angular speed is obtained,

$$\dot{\Phi}_{t+1} = \dot{\Phi}_t + J^{-1}\left(\dot{p}_f - \dot{p}_t\right) \tag{15}$$

where $\mathbf{p}_t$ is the actual robot 3D position and $\mathbf{p}_f$ represents the final desired position in space. To achieve such location, the robot recursively approximates the next desired rotor's controlled velocity. The next figure depicts a simulation result where the aerial robot successively approached the final desired position, staring from the Cartesian origin.

4. Aerodynamic robot's model

The aerodynamic robot's model refers to the application of the Newton's second law of motion in three dimensions to infer the thrusting force T and other involved forces that produce the Cartesian accelerations:

$$\begin{aligned} \ddot{x} = {} & \ddot{d}c_1s_0 - \dot{d}s_1s_0\dot{\phi}_1 + \dot{d}c_1c_0\dot{\phi}_0 + \dot{d}c_1c_0\phi_1 - ds_1c_0\dot{\phi}_0\dot{\phi}_1 - dc_1c_0\dot{\phi}_0^2 \\ & -dc_1c_0\ddot{\phi}_0 - \dot{d}s_1s_0\dot{\phi}_1 - dc_1s_0\dot{\phi}_1^2 - ds_1c_0\dot{\phi}_1\dot{\phi}_0 - ds_1s_0\ddot{\phi}_1 \end{aligned} \tag{16}$$

$$\ddot{y} = \ddot{d}s_1 + dc_1\dot{\phi}_1 + \dot{d}c_1\phi_1 - ds_1\dot{\phi}_1^2 + dc_1\ddot{\phi}_1 \tag{17}$$

$$\begin{aligned} \ddot{z} = {} & \ddot{d}c_1c_0 - \dot{d}s_1c_0\dot{\phi}_1 - \dot{d}c_1s_0\dot{\phi}_0 - ds_1c_0\phi_1 - dc_1c_0\dot{\phi}_1^2 + ds_1s_0\dot{\phi}_0\dot{\phi}_1 \\ & -ds_1c_0\ddot{\phi}_1 - \dot{d}c_1s_0\dot{\phi}_0 + \dot{d}s_1s_0\dot{\phi}_0\dot{\phi}_1 - dc_1c_0\dot{\phi}_0^2 - dc_1s_0\ddot{\phi}_0 \end{aligned} \tag{18}$$

In the matrix form, the following equation represents the direct kinematic solution for the Cartesian accelerations:

$$\ddot{p} = \begin{pmatrix} dc_1c_0 & -ds_1s_0 & c_1s_0 \\ 0 & dc_1 & s_1 \\ -dc_1c_0 & -ds_1c_0 & c_1s_0 \end{pmatrix} \begin{pmatrix} \dot{\phi}_0 \\ \dot{\phi}_1 \\ \dot{d} \end{pmatrix} + \begin{pmatrix} -dc_1c_0 & -dc_1c_0 & -2dc_1c_0 & 2dc_1c_0 & -2ds_1s_0 \\ 0 & -ds_1 & 0 & 0 & 2c_1 \\ -dc_1c_0 & -dc_1c_0 & -2ds_1s_0 & 2dc_1s_0 & -2ds_1c_0 \end{pmatrix} \tag{19}$$

or

$$\ddot{p} = J_1 \cdot \dot{\Phi} + J_2 \cdot \dot{\Phi}$$

From the previous expression, the vector acceleration is substituted into the Newton's second law of motion,

$$f = m \cdot \ddot{p} \tag{20}$$

where the Cartesian force components defined in robot's local inertial frame are expressed as follows:

$$f_x = T\cos(\theta_1)\sin(\theta_0) \tag{21}$$

The force component along the robot's local y component is expressed as

$$f_y = T\sin(\theta_1) \tag{22}$$

And, the force component along the robot's local Z component is expressed as

$$f_z = T\cos(\theta_1)\cos(\theta_0) \tag{23}$$

By simplifying the Cartesian force components in the matrix form

$$f = T\begin{pmatrix} c_1 s_0 \\ s_1 \\ c_1 c_0 \end{pmatrix} \tag{24}$$

And, by substituting the functional form of the vector force f into the Newton's second law,

$$m \cdot \ddot{p} = T\begin{pmatrix} c_1 s_0 \\ s_1 \\ c_1 c_0 \end{pmatrix} \tag{25}$$

Thus, by reordering the previous equation, we substitute the vector constraints $\mathbf{w}^{\mathrm{T}} = (C_1S_0, S_1, C_1C_0)$. The acceleration vector $d^2\mathbf{p}/dt^2$ is a function of the next position $\mathbf{p}_{t+1}$ and the rotors variables:

$$Tw = m\ddot{p}\left(p_{t+1}, \Phi_f, \dot{\Phi}_t\right) \tag{26}$$

By dropping off the induced robot's force T,

$$T = w^{-1} m\ddot{p}\left(p_{t+1}, \Phi_f, \dot{\Phi}_t\right) \tag{27}$$

So far, in this expression, the total thrusting induced force T represents the robot's global flying force. Thus, T is an arithmetic result produced by the sum of the top rotor's induced force T_1 and the below rotor's induced force T_2 according to the following governing constraints:

(a) For $T_1 = T_2$, the inflow air mass is same throughout both rotors, hence $T = T_1 + T_2$.

(b) For $T_1 > T_2$, speed and air mass below rotor 1 are greater than rotor 2 inflow, $T = T_1 + \alpha_2 T_2$.

(c) For $T_1<T_2$, opposed to constraint (b), then $T_2 = \alpha_2 T_1$ and $T = T_1(1+\alpha_2)$.

Here, the numerical factors $\alpha_{1,2}$ are gains denoting rotors' speed-rate differences. For either constraint (b) or (c), the gyroscopic mechanism angles' tilt and pitch are affected, consequently changing the robot's azimuth and elevation angles.

5. Induced force model

According to the depictions of **Figure 3**, the rotors are continuously pushing the air down. As per Newton's third law, an equal and opposite reaction force, denoted as rotor thrust, is acting on the rotor due to air. The induced force model refers to the thrusting force exerted to accelerate the robot. And at a constant velocity the quasi-static hovering is achieved [1–4].

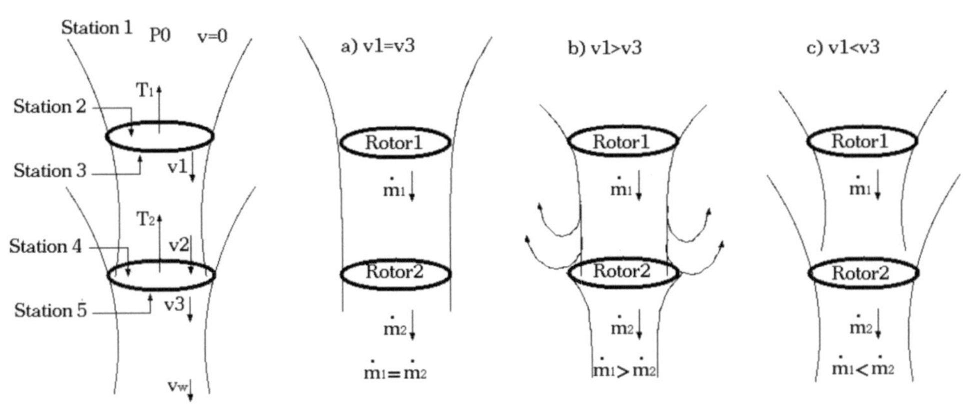

Figure 3. Rotors' flow conditions in the slip streams.

The momentum conservation is obtained by relating the induced force T_2 to the rate of momentum change. It is the mass rate and the far-field wake-induced velocity v_w below rotor 2, where $dm/dt = \varrho A v_2$ and the rotor disk area $A = \pi R^2$. Thus, the moment conservation

$$T = \dot{m} v_w \tag{28}$$

The energy conservation per unit time

$$Tv = \frac{1}{2}\dot{m} v_w^2 \tag{29}$$

To obtain a relationship between v and v_w, let us substitute T and dm/dt,

$$\dot{m} v_w v = \frac{1}{2}\dot{m} v_w^2 \tag{30}$$

http://dx.doi.org/10.5772/63548

Algebraically simplifying,

$$v = \frac{1}{2}v_w; v_w = 2v \tag{31}$$

Hence, substituting v_w into T,

$$T = \dot{m}v_w = 2\dot{m}v \tag{32}$$

Then,

$$T = 2\rho A v^2 \tag{33}$$

Dropping off v, the following expression is obtained;

$$v = \sqrt{\frac{T}{2\rho A}} \tag{34}$$

The propulsive power P_w is the thrusting force T capable to move the robot at a given velocity (distance over time):

$$P_w = Tv = T\sqrt{\frac{T}{2\rho A}} \tag{35}$$

The induced power per unit thrust for a hovering rotor can be written as

$$\frac{P_w}{T} = v = \sqrt{\frac{T}{2\rho A}} \tag{36}$$

The above expression indicates that, for a low inflow velocity, the efficiency is higher. This is possible if the rotor has a low disk loading (T/A). Note that the parameter determining the induced power is essentially $T/(A)$. Therefore, the effective disk loading increases with an increase in altitude and temperature.

From previous analysis, let us now precisely define the thrusting force for rotors 1 and 2, according to **Figure 3** (left side). For rotor 1, the air mass flow is

$$\dot{m}_1 = \rho A_1 v_1 \tag{37}$$

Hence, considering only rotor 1, the induced force is

$$T_1 = \dot{m}_1 v_2 \tag{38}$$

The energy conservation principle for rotor 1 is expressed as

$$T_1 v_1 = \frac{1}{2} \dot{m}_1 v_2^2 \tag{39}$$

And finding a relationship between v_1 and v_2 in accordance with **Figure 3** (left side),

$$v_2 = 2v_1 \tag{40}$$

Thus,

$$T_1 = 2\rho_1 A_1 v_1^2 \tag{41}$$

The induced air velocity induced by rotor 1 is modelled by

$$v_1 = \sqrt{\frac{T_1}{2\rho_1 A_1}} \tag{42}$$

Similarly, modelling both the induced force T_2 and velocity v_2 for rotor 2, the following analysis is developed. The airflow rate,

$$\dot{m}_2 = \rho_2 A_2 v_3 \tag{43}$$

And the induced force T_2 considers the inflow air mass and the far-field wake-induced velocity v_w,

$$T_2 = \dot{m}_2 v_w \tag{44}$$

The energy conservation for the second rotor is expressed as

$$T_2 v_3 = \frac{1}{2} \dot{m}_2 v_w^2 \tag{45}$$

The relationship between far-field wake-induced air velocity v_w and v_3 is given by v_w=$2v_3$, and

$$T_2 = 2\rho_2 A_2 v_3^2 \tag{46}$$

Therefore, the second rotor's air induced velocity is

$$v_3 = \sqrt{\frac{T_2}{2\rho_2 A_2}} \tag{47}$$

From the three previous postulates of **Figure 3**, let us deduce the conditions when both rotors, although asynchronous, simultaneously induce the airflow equally, when v_1=v_3 (**Figure 3a**). For this case, the total robot's thrusting force T=T_1+T_2,

$$T = 2\rho_1 A_1 v_1^2 + 2\rho_2 A_2 v_3^2 \tag{48}$$

For case 1, let us assume A_1=A_2 and v_2=v_3 through the second rotor's disc area. And,

$$v_w = 2v_3; likewise, v_2 = 2v_1; hencev_w = 2(2v_1) = 4v_1 \tag{49}$$

Rewriting total T as a function of v_1, thus we have

$$\rho_2 = \frac{m_c}{v_c} \tag{50}$$

The air mass variation is denoted as the mass derivative w.r.t. time,

$$\dot{m} = \rho_2 A V_2 \tag{51}$$

Now, for the case v_1>v_3,

$$T = T_1 + \alpha_2 T_2 \tag{52}$$

Let us substitute our T_1 and T_2 models previously analysed,

$$T = 2\rho_1 A_1 v_1^2 + 2\rho_2 A_2 v_3^2 \tag{53}$$

In addition, A_1=A_2, v_2=2v_1 and v_w=2v_3, but v_2>v_3 hence v_3=$\alpha_2 v_2$. Thus, v_w=2(α_2 2(2v_1)), and we obtain the relationship between the far-field wake-induced velocity and v_1:

$$v_w = 6\alpha_2 v_1 \tag{54}$$

By substituting v_1 into expression T, developing and factorising algebraically,

$$T = 2Av_1^2 \left(\rho_1 + 4\alpha_2 \rho_2\right) \tag{55}$$

Similarly, for the case when v_1<v_3, T=T_1(1+α_2),

$$T = 2\rho_1 A_1 v_1^2 + 2\rho_2 A_2 v_3^2 \tag{56}$$

for this case, A_1=A_2, v_2=$2v_1$ and v_w=$2v_3$. However, just above and below rotor 2, v_2<v_3, and therefore v_2=$\alpha_2 v_3$, then v_3=$2v_2/\alpha_2$.

$$T = 2\rho_1 A v_1^2 + 2\rho_2 A\left(2\frac{v_1}{\alpha_2}\right)^2 \tag{57}$$

Factorizing and algebraically arranging,

$$T = 2Av_1^2\left(\rho_1 + \frac{8\rho_2}{\alpha_2^2}\right) \tag{58}$$

Solving the parameter α_2 for each of the three cases,

$$\alpha_2^2 = \begin{cases} 4, & v_1 = v_3 \\ 1, & v_1 > v_3 \\ \sqrt{2}, & v1 < v_3 \end{cases} \tag{59}$$

Therefore, we synthesise the total thrusting force T for all cases by

$$T = 2Av_1^2\left(\rho_1 + \alpha_2^2\rho_2\right) \tag{60}$$

Therefore, from Eq. (60), now we have a functional form for the thrusting force T. Thus, to reach a controlled rotors' velocity, we must establish a relationship between the induced velocity v_1 and the rotor angular velocity $d\phi/dt$ using the tip speed of the rotor blade as reference. The rotor inflow is represented in non-dimensional form as

$$\lambda = \frac{v_3}{\dot{\phi}R} = \sqrt{\frac{C_T}{2}} \tag{61}$$

where C_T is the thrust coefficient modelled by

$$C_T = \frac{T}{\rho_2 A(\dot{\phi}_t R)^2} \tag{62}$$

http://dx.doi.org/10.5772/63548

Therefore, the following equality allow us to deduce C_T with more

$$\dot{\phi} = \frac{v_1}{R\sqrt{\frac{C_T}{2}}} \tag{63}$$

Thus, substituting (Texto) into v_1,

$$v_1 = \left(\dot{\phi} R\sqrt{\frac{C_T}{2}}\right)^2 \tag{64}$$

And subsequently, v_1^2 is substituted into T,

$$T = A(\dot{\phi}^2 R^2 C_T)(\rho_1 + \alpha_2^2 \rho_2) \tag{65}$$

Therefore, the induced force T arising from the fluid mechanics equation (65) is equated with the induced force of the flight mechanics equation (27), the following expression is obtained:

$$2A\left(\dot{\phi}^2 R^2 \frac{C_T}{2}\right)(\rho_1 + \alpha_2^2 \rho_2) = w^{-1} m\ddot{p} \tag{66}$$

Our objective is to find an analytical solution for the rotor speed required to reach the induced velocity v_1 and the induced force T, which is governed by the flight mechanics law. The induced air mass velocity v_1 can be expressed in terms of the rotor speed that is controlled to obtain the desired angular velocity,

$$\dot{\phi} = \sqrt{\frac{m w^{-1} \ddot{p}}{A R^2 C_T (\rho_1 + \alpha_2^2 \rho_2)}} \tag{67}$$

This model represents the independent variable to control the motors' Speed of Eq. (73) or Eq. (74):

Thus, it follows a set of empirical temperature measurements where some experimental hovering experiments were carried out. The plots in **Figure 4** depict how the air pressure is affected as the temperature varies over time.

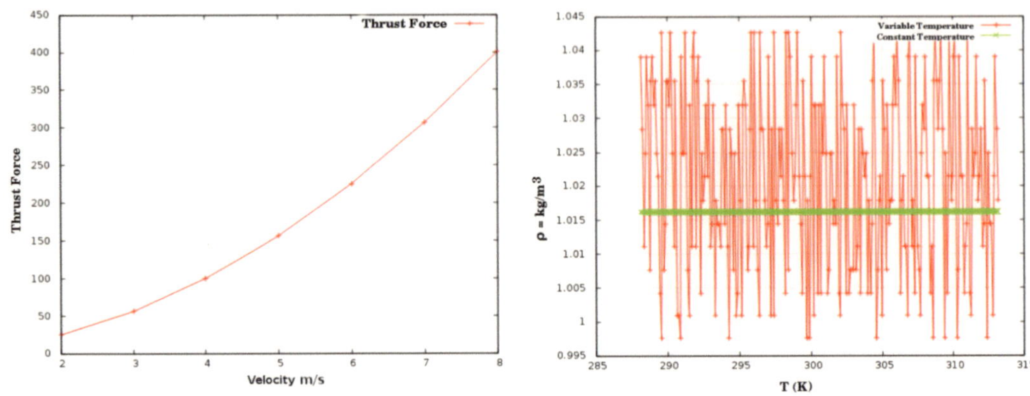

Figure 4. Left: Thrusting force w.r.t. induced velocity. Right: Air mass density as temperature varies.

6. Actuators' speed model

The actuators' self-calibration speed model is discussed in this section. The real rotary velocity in a range from minimal to maximal values approached a logarithmic model. It considered the empirical set of angular speed measurements w.r.t. digital controls. The inherent physical variations, such as temperature, air pressure, density and air dust particles, affected the actuators' performance. Since the angular speed value capable to hover the spherical robot's body is disturbed, a self-calibration is required to maintain position control as accurate as possible. From experiments, the empirical models that obtained (**Figure 5**) φ vs. d are fitted according to the next model. The parameters A and β are unknown and must fit the speed measurements φ, w.r.t to digital word d,

$$\dot{\phi} = A + \beta ln(d) \tag{68}$$

We temporally substitute d'=ln(d), and thus the rotary speed

$$\dot{\phi} = A = \beta d' \tag{69}$$

To estimate the unknown parameter β, a linear mean-squared method is applied,

$$\beta = \frac{n\left(\sum d'\dot{\phi} - (\sum d')(\sum \dot{\phi})\right)}{n(\sum d'^2) - (\sum d')^2} \tag{70}$$

Subsequently, the previous parameter solution is used in the next expression A,

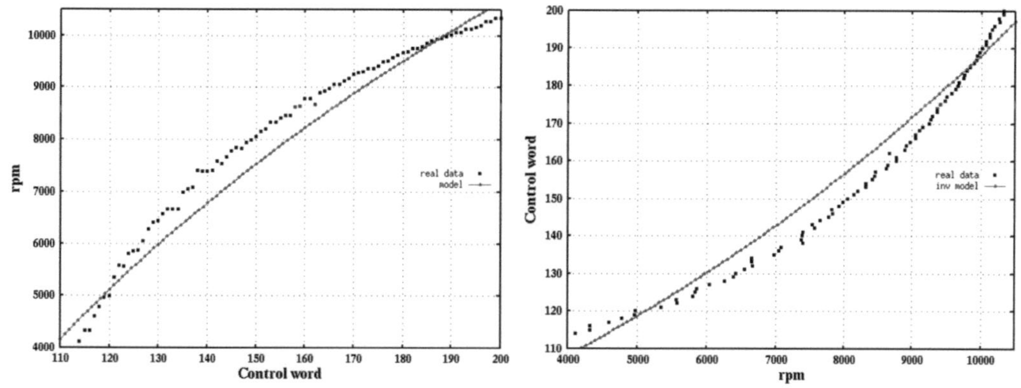

Figure 5. Actuator's raw measurements. Left: Direct solution. Right: Inverse solution.

$$A = \frac{\sum \dot{\phi}}{n} - \beta \frac{\sum d'}{n} \tag{71}$$

By substituting the parameters numerical values, the rotary speed model is obtained as follows:

$$\dot{\phi} = 10838.57637 ln(d) - 46776.63059 \tag{72}$$

In addition, in order to obtain the inverse solution, we algebraically drop off the variable *d* from Eq. (72),

$$d = e^{\frac{\dot{\phi} - A}{\beta}} \tag{73}$$

And numerical parametric values from Eq. (72) are substituted into (73) to obtain

$$d = e^{\frac{\dot{\phi} - 46776.6306}{10838.5764}} \tag{74}$$

In order to compare how our theoretical model fits the empirical model, both inverse and direct operation control modes are depicted in **Figure 5**.

7. Rotor's speed control

From the previous section, the actuators' speed model is now used to formulate a feedback linear control. Let us assume that a rotor control variable (i.e., angle, velocity and acceleration) should ideally be equal to the real sensed control variable, as expressed by the next equality (75). Nevertheless, in a realistic scenario real and ideal control variables are different due to a number of factors, such as frictions, inertial and gravity forces, motor electromagnetic performance and so on. Thus, both variables are approached by a multiplicative gain or factor alpha, which approximates both numerical values according to the relation

$$\varphi = k\hat{\phi} \tag{75}$$

Assuming an arbitrary actual derivative order, the equation is equivalently expressed as

$$\frac{d}{dt}\varphi = k\frac{d}{dt}\phi \tag{76}$$

The time differentials are eliminated and the remaining differentials are obtained by solving the following definite integrals,

$$\int_{\varphi_1}^{\varphi_2} d\,\varphi = k\int_{\phi_1}^{\phi_2} d\,\phi \tag{77}$$

By solving the definite integrals,

$$\varphi_2 - \varphi_1 = k(\phi_2 - \phi_1) \tag{78}$$

In this case, $\hat{\varphi}_2$ is the expected or the reference value to be reached ideally, $\hat{\varphi}_2=\varphi^{\mathrm{ref}}$. Thus, by adjusting the times sub-interval labels, and algebraically reordering, the next recursive numerical successive approximation equation is expressed as follows:

$$\varphi_{t+1} = \varphi_t + k\left(\varphi^{ref} - \phi_t\right) = \varphi_t + ke_t \tag{79}$$

From the previous expression, the error ke_t is spanned into the past (angular displacement), the actual (rotary speed) and the future (angular accelerations) errors in order to cover the whole error history. And the general constant gain k is proportional to k_p, k_I and k_d. Thus,

$$\varphi_{t+1} = \varphi_t + \left(k_p e_p + k_I e_I + k_d e_d\right) \tag{80}$$

Therefore, the next feedback proportional error e_p (rad/s) with proportional gain k_p (dimensionless) is obtained with the observation ϕ_t measured online. And the reference model (Texto) is established in terms of the instantaneous control word δ_t:

$$k_p e_p = k_p\left(\dot{\phi}^{ref} - \dot{\phi}_t\right) = k_p\left(a ln(\delta) - b - \dot{\phi}_t\right) \tag{81}$$

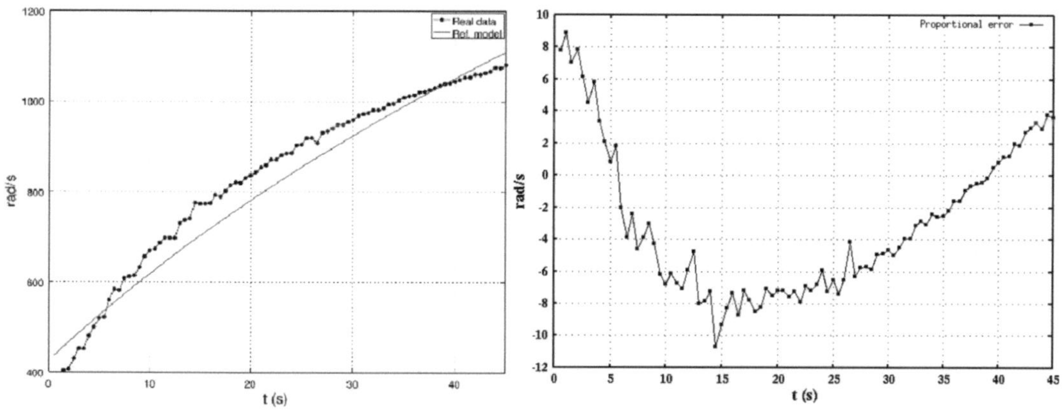

Figure 6. Left: Measurement and reference proportional models. Right: Proportional error.

For illustrative purpose, an accelerative rotor's task to exert robot's propulsion was performed. **Figure 6** (left) depicts both the reference model ϕ^{ref} and the observation $\phi(t)$.

In addition, **Figure 6** (right) shows the proportional error behaviour ϕ^{ref}-$\phi(t)$ without k_p. Furthermore, the feedback integral error e_I (rad/s) with integral gain k_I (dimensionless) is expressed by the time integration of the difference of $(d^2\phi/dt^2 - d^2\phi(t)/dt^2)$.

$$k_I e_I = k_I \left(\int \left(\ddot{\phi}^{ref} - \ddot{\phi}_t \right) dt \right) \tag{82}$$

The observation model $d^2\phi/dt^2$ was obtained online by the numerical derivatives of the optical encoder according to the following relationship:

$$\ddot{\phi}(t) = \frac{\dot{\phi}_{t_2} - \dot{\phi}_{t_1}}{t_2 - t_1} \tag{83}$$

In addition, since the observation model inherently poses perturbations, an analytical reference model $d^2\phi^{ref}/dt^2$ was obtained using a nonlinear regressive fitting process for parameters identification,

$$\begin{pmatrix} \sum \ddot{\phi}_i \\ \sum \ddot{\phi}\, t_i \\ \sum \ddot{\phi}_i\, t_i^2 \end{pmatrix} = \begin{pmatrix} n & \sum t_i & \sum t_i^2 \\ \sum t_i & \sum t_i^2 & \sum t_i^3 \\ \sum t_i^2 & \sum t_i^3 & \sum t_i^4 \end{pmatrix} \cdot \begin{pmatrix} a_0 \\ a_1 \\ a_2 \end{pmatrix} \tag{84}$$

where the previous expression is similarly expressed as

$$y = A \cdot x \tag{85}$$

And by solving vector **x**,

$$x = A^{-1} \cdot y \tag{86}$$

Hence, the reference model is a theoretical nonlinear function of time,

$$\ddot{\phi}^{ref}(t) = 34.7950 - 1.2832t + 0.0145t^2 \tag{87}$$

Therefore, for the sake of the integral control u_I (rad/s), the angular acceleration reference model (Texto) is substituted next in its general form:

$$u_I = k_I\left(\int (a_0 - a_{1t} + a_2t^2) - \ddot{\phi}(t)dt\right) \tag{88}$$

Finally, in order to keep data homogeneity (numerical data subtraction), time integration is obtained by the trapezoid rule for numerical integration,

$$\dot{\phi}_k = \frac{t_f - t_0}{2n}\left[\left(\ddot{\phi}_0^{ref} - \ddot{\phi}_0(t)\right) + 2\sum\left(\ddot{\phi}_t^{ref} - \ddot{\phi}_t\right) + \left(\ddot{\phi}_{t_f}^{ref}(t) - \ddot{\phi}_{t_f}(t)\right)\right] \tag{89}$$

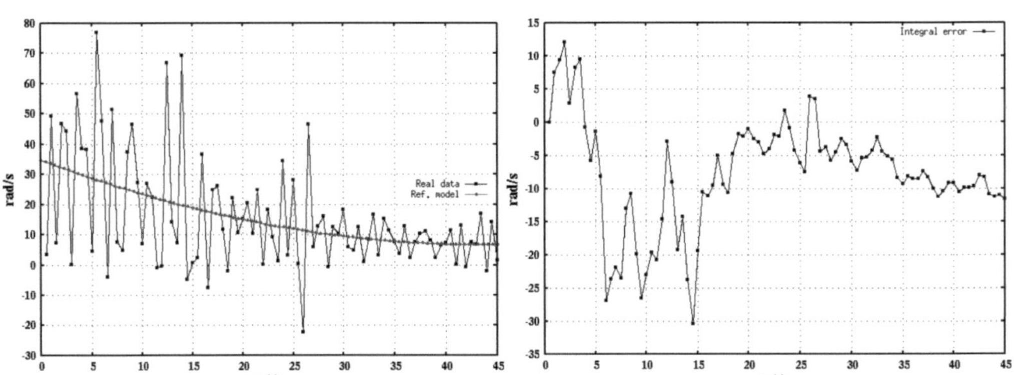

Figure 7. Left: Measurement and reference integral models. Right: Integral error.

Figure 7 (left) depicts both reference and empirical models integrated with time. **Figure 7** (right) shows the integral error behaviour.

In addition, the derivative control $u_d = k_d e_d$ (rad/s) with feedback derivative error e_d, and with derivative gain k_d (dimensionless), improves the closed-loop stability as follows:

$$k_d e_d = k_d\left(\frac{d}{dt}\phi^{\text{ref}} - \frac{d}{dt}\phi_t\right) \tag{90}$$

http://dx.doi.org/10.5772/63548

In order to obtain the time derivative observation model, the rotor's angle evolution $\phi(t)$ (rad) is observed online using an optical encoder during the time slot where velocity and acceleration are also measured. As the measurements are read with noise, the analytical reference model is fitted as a nonlinear polynomial of the following form:

$$\phi^{\text{ref}}(t) = -3709.6273 + 2116.9484t + 27.9289t^2 \tag{91}$$

where the derivative error general form is expressed as

$$k_d e_d = k_d \frac{d}{dt}\left(-b_0 + b_{1t} + b_2 t^2 - \phi(t)\right) \tag{92}$$

Figure 8 (left) depicts both reference $\phi^{\text{ref}}(t)$ and observation $\phi(t)$ models together. Although both curves are apparently fitted, the vertical scale is provided in thousands of radians. **Figure 8** (right) shows the derivative error scale.

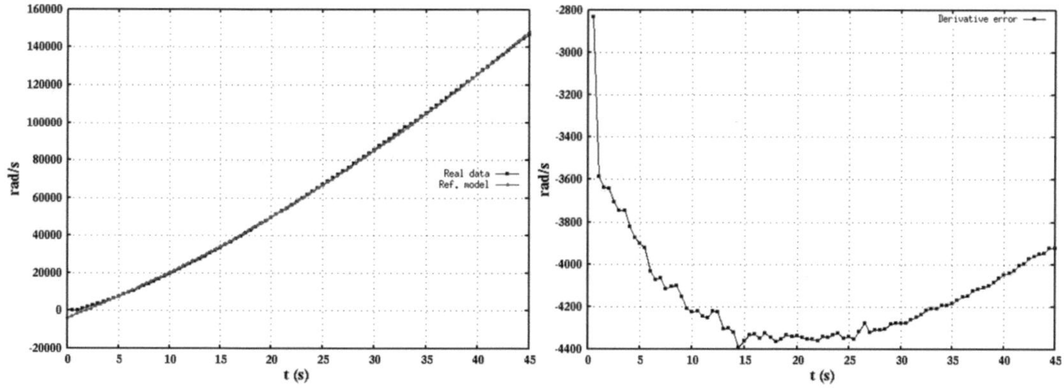

Figure 8. Left: Measurement and reference derivative models. Right: Derivative error.

Generally, the PID controller is expressed by the next expression

$$u_t = k_p\left((a\ln(d) - b) - \dot{\phi}_i\right) + k_I\left(\int_t \left(a_0 - a_{1t} + a_{2t}^2 - \ddot{\phi}_t\right) dt\right) + k_d\left(\frac{d}{dt}\left(-b_0 + b_{1t} + b_{2t}^2 - \phi(t)\right)\right) \tag{93}$$

Therefore, the controlled rotor's velocity that is recursively calculated by $d\varphi_{t+1}/dt = d\varphi_t/dt + u_t$ is applied, and we established the following controller choices: proportional (P), proportional integral (PI) and proportional-integral-derivative. **Figure 9** (left) depicts the rotors' angular speed without control and with three types of controllers. The constant parameters were adjusted accordingly to obtain such results. We can see that after 25 s the responses P and PI gradually converge w.r.t. the raw rotor's speed (**Figure 9**, left).

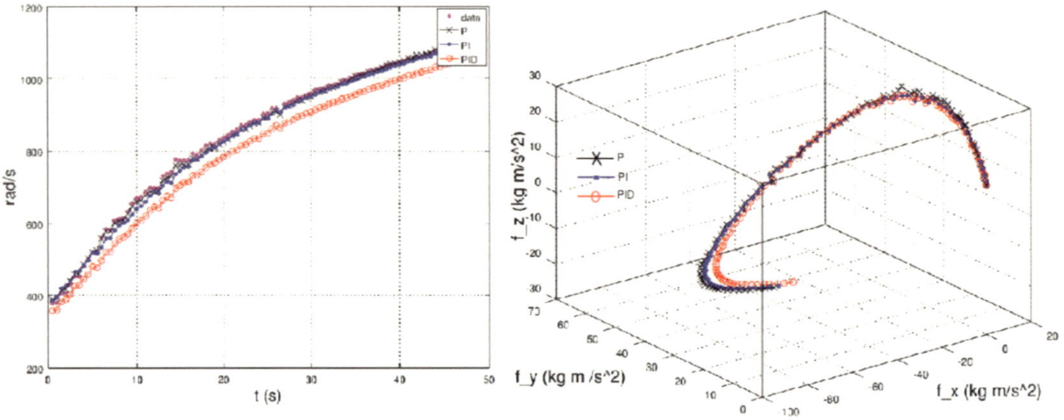

Figure 9. Controllers P, PI and PID. Left: Rotor's angular speed. Right: Induced Cartesian forces.

In addition, with the controlled rotor's speed output, the induced force is iteratively calculated by

$$T(\dot{\varphi}_{t+1}) = A\dot{\varphi}_{t+1}^2 R^2 C_T(\rho_1 + \alpha_2^2 \rho_2) \tag{94}$$

Thus, **Figure 9** (right) depicts the induced component forces that are produced using three types of controllers.

8. Conclusions

This work briefly introduced the design of an aerial spherical robot with under-actuated gyroscopic mechanism. Although the purpose of this study was not to describe the robot flying and physical capabilities, the main objective was to demonstrate the induced force model deploying dual collinear rotary wings with no steering actuators. This study describes the following four major areas: the robot flight mechanics, the model of the induced thrusting forces, the self-calibration actuators' Speed model validated with three types of controllers (P, PI, PID) to drive the rotors' motor speed. The proposed aerodynamic mechanism poses neither ailerons nor propellers for steering control. Although the platform is a home-made laboratory prototype with special arrangements, the main focus of this chapter is to model the hypothesis of controlling the robot's directions by varying rotors' asynchronous speed. To achieve this, the under-actuated gyroscopic mechanism provides the ability to control its inner yaw, pitch and roll angles. Until this stage, the robot development is under an early control capability. However, this study presents mathematical solutions and simulation results to demonstrate the proposed aerodynamic hypothesis.

Author details

G. Santos-Medina, K.Y. Heras-Gaytán, E.A. Martínez-García*, R. Torres-Córdoba and V. Carrillo-Saucedo

*Address all correspondence to: edmartin@uacj.mx

Laboratorio de Robótica, Institute of Engineering and Technology, Universidad Autónoma de Ciudad Juárez Ave. Del Charro, Cd. Juarez, Chihuahua, Mexico

References

[1] Venkatesan C. Fundamentals of helicopter dynamics. CRC Press Taylor and Francis Group; 2015.

[2] Stepniewski W, Keys C. Rotary-wing aerodynamics. New York: Dover Publications; 1984.

[3] Johnson W. Helicopter theory. New York: Dover Publications; 1994.

[4] Seddon J, Newman S. Basic helicopter aerodynamics. Chichester, England: Wiley; 2011.

[5] Briod A, Kornatowski P, Zufferey J, Floreano DA. Collision-resilient flying robot. Journal of Field Robotics, 31(4), 496–509, 2013.

[6] Dudley C, A Spherical Aerial Terrestrial Robot, MSc Thesis, University of Nevada, Reno, 2014.

[7] Briod A, Klaptocz A, Zufferey J-C, Floreano D. The AirBurr: a flying robot that can exploit collisions. International Conference on Complex Medical Engineering, Japan, pp. 569–574, 2012.

[8] Alkalla MG, Fanni MA, Mohamed M.A novel propeller-type climbing robot for vessels inspection. IEEE International Conference on Advanced Intelligent Mechatronics, South Korea, pp.1623–1628, 2015.

[9] Mizutani S,Okada Y,Salaan CJ,Ishii T,Ohno K,Tadokoro S. Proposal and experimental validation of a design strategy for a UAV with a passive rotating spherical shell. IEEE/RSJ IROS, Germany, pp. 1271–1278, 2015.

[10] Czyba R, Szafranski G, Janik M, Pampuch K, Hecel M, Development of co-axial Y6-Rotor UAV—design, mathematical modeling, rapid prototyping and experimental

validation. International Conference on Unmanned Aircraft Systems, USA, pp. 1102–1111, 2015.

[11] Kawasaki K, Zhao M, Okada K, Inaba M. MUWA: multi-field universal wheel for air-land vehicle with quad variable-pitch propellers. IEEE/RSJ IROS, Japan, pp. 1880–1885, 2013.

[12] Ho-Joon L, Han-Woong A, Jae-Kwang L, Ju L, Sung-Hong W. Newly proposed hybrid type mutli-DOF operation motor for multi-copter UAV systems. IEEE Energy Conversion Congress and Exposition, Canada, pp. 2782–2790, 2015.

[13] Zhang W, Fan N, Wang Z, Wu Y, Modeling and aerodynamic analysis of a ducted-fan micro aerial vehicle. International Conference on Modelling, Identification & Control, China, pp. 768–773, 2012.

Chapter 3

Adaptive Steering and Trajectory Control of Wheeled Mobile Robots for Autonomous Navigation

Mariam Al-Sagban and Rached Dhaouadi

Additional information is available at the end of the chapter

http://dx.doi.org/10.5772/64227

Abstract

This chapter presents a new reactive navigation algorithm for a wheeled mobile robot (WMR) with a differential drive mechanism moving in unknown environments [1]. The mobile robot is controlled to travel to a predefined goal position safely and efficiently without any prior map of the environment. The navigation is achieved by modulating the steering angle and turning radius. To avoid obstacles while seeking the goal position, the dimensions and shape of the robot are incorporated to determine the set of all possible collision-free steering angles. The algorithm then selects the optimum steering angle candidate to contour the obstacle. Simulation and experimental results on a WMR prototype are used to validate the proposed algorithms.

Keywords: recurrent neural networks, obstacle avoidance, robots

1. Introduction

Over the years, mobile robots have evolved rapidly incorporating a wide spectrum of applications. They aid within the field of medical technologies, assist in vehicle driving, and can be occupied for use within hazardous rescue missions. Mobile robots helped monitor the spread of oil during the catastrophic spill on the Gulf of Mexico [2]. Additionally, robots were of great aid during the Japanese Fukushima nuclear crisis in monitoring the radiation levels and cleaning up leftover debris [3].

In performing all previous tasks, mobile robots must be equipped with autonomous navigation. This is described as the arrival at of the robot at a target location without any assistance, and whilst avoiding obstacles present around. Perception, path planning, localization, and motion control are the key elements that build toward autonomous navigation. With perception, sensors pick up information regarding the robots immediate environment that are then perceived and translated within the robot. The next step is path planning, which is the robot's ability to come to a consensus regarding the required action as a result of its expected goal. The final step occurs with motion control through which the robot executes the required action through its actuators [4].

In this chapter, we focus on path planning in unknown environments [5]. Path planning represents a key feature of autonomous navigation. The problem of path planning is usually classified in three categories according to the given environment and constraints:

- Global Path Planning—This framework requires full knowledge of the robot workspace; a global map is supplied as given input.
- Local Path Planning (Sensor-Based Path Planning)—This framework requires partial knowledge of the workspace. Therefore, only an incomplete map is supplied.
- Reactive Navigation (Obstacle Avoidance)—In this framework, no a priori information is required about the workspace. Instead, obstacles are discovered in real time while the robot is executing its motion.

Due to the inherent nature of the obstacle avoidance problem, navigation algorithms do not produce efficient paths and do not guarantee global convergence as would global path planning algorithms. This would result the robot in producing inefficient paths or failing to reach the goal position (trap position).

The implementation of path planning and obstacle avoidance techniques on a real mobile robot imposes different types of constraints including kinematic, dynamic, and time constraints. The differential drive robot must follow a curve path due to the kinematic constraint as it is unable to reach the desired point place instantly and in a short period of time. Disregarding this limitation, when dealing with path planning and obstacle avoidance techniques, would lead to an unsafe design as the transitional curve may potentially intersect with obstacles and, therefore, result in a collision.

2. Autonomous navigation concepts

2.1. The configuration space

For a two-dimensional robot, the robot configuration can be fully described by rigidly attaching a frame to the robot and then specifying the position and orientation of this frame in the global frame. The complete specification of the location of every point on the robot is called a configuration, q. The set of all possible configurations is called a configuration space or C-space ($q \in \mathcal{C}$). A rigid object moving in a plane is, therefore, specified by the triple configuration, $q = (x, y, \theta)$, and the configuration space can be represented by $\mathcal{C} = \mathbb{R}^2 \times SO(2)$, where $SO(2)$ is the special orthogonal group of 2-D rotations [6].

http://dx.doi.org/10.5772/64227

The introduction of new notation is important for the description of collisions. The workspace in which the robot moves will be denoted as $\mathcal{W}$. When the robot moves in a plane, the workspace is now denoted as $W = \mathbb{R}^2$. The subset of this workspace occupied by obstacles is then denoted as $\mathcal{O} \subset \mathcal{W}$, and the subset occupied by the robot at configuration is denoted as $\mathcal{A}(q) \subset \mathcal{W}$. The robot must avoid a configuration causing it to come into physical contact with any obstacle, as this would cause a collision otherwise. The set of configurations in which the robot would come into a collision with an obstacle is defined as the obstacle configuration space,

$$\mathcal{C}_{obst} = \{q \in \mathcal{C} \mid \mathcal{A}(q) \bigcap \mathcal{O} = \emptyset\}. \tag{1}$$

On the other hand, the set of all collision-free configurations is defined as the free configuration space. It is defined as the set difference

$$\mathcal{C}_{free} = \mathcal{C} \setminus \mathcal{C}_{obst} \tag{2}$$

The configuration space of a rigid robot translating in the plane $\mathcal{W} = \mathbb{R}^2$ is two-dimensional, easily visualized in **Figure 1**. The circular-shape robot is presented with an obstacle in the workspace. When sliding the robot around the obstacle, the boundary configuration can be determined. As a result, motion planning for the robot in the workspace is converted to motion planning for a point robot in the configuration space [7].

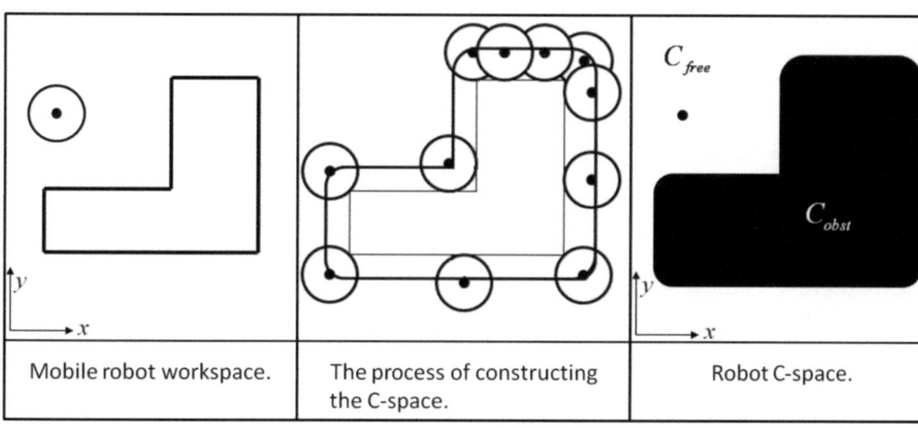

Figure 1. Construction of the configuration space.

2.2. Definition of obstacle avoidance

Let q_{target} be a target configuration. At time t_i the robot is in configuration $q(t_i)$. The robot senses a portion of the environment using its onboard sensors. Let the set of workspace obstacles seen at configuration $q(t_i)$ be $\mathcal{O}(q(t_i)) \subset \mathcal{W}$. The objective is to compute a motion control vector u_i such that

- The robot progresses to the target location $F(q(t_i), q_{\text{target}}) < F(q(t_i + T), q_{\text{target}})$, where $F: \mathcal{C} \times \mathcal{C} \rightarrow \mathbb{R}^+$ is a function that evaluates the progress of one configuration to another [8].
- The trajectory does not collide with the obstacles $\mathcal{A}(Q_{t_i,T}) \cap \mathcal{O}(q(t_i)) = \emptyset$, where $Q_{t_i,T}$ is the set of configurations of the trajectory followed from $q(t_i)$ to $q(t_i + T)$. $T > 0$ is the sampling period.

The solution of the problem is a sequence of control vectors $\{u_1, \ldots, u_n\}$ computed in real time that guide the robot eventually to the target configuration while avoiding the sensed obstacles in the environment as shown in **Figure 2**.

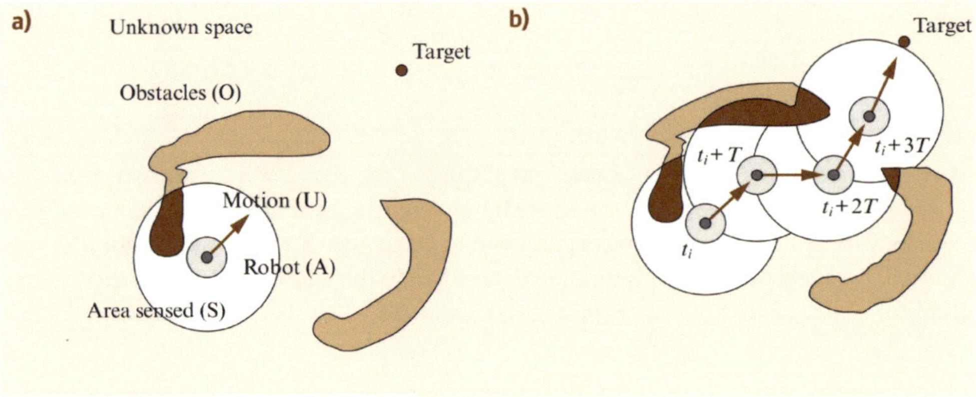

Figure 2. Obstacle avoidance problem [8].

2.3. Kinematics of a two-wheel differential drive robot

A differential drive robot is composed of one passive wheel and two coaxial wheels. The passive wheel provides stability, while the coaxial pair steer the robot through carefully modulating their velocities. A straight line motion is achieved through equal velocities in both wheels, while left and right motion occurs if the right wheel is faster than the left and the left wheel is faster than the right, respectively. Pivoting is noticed when both wheels steer equally as fast, but in opposite directions. A zero turning radius is a major advantage with this motion configuration. An initial rotation can trigger motion in any direction. Further advantages to this robot configuration include the simple mechanical structure and kinematic model and the low fabrication cost. However, this robot configuration has also a few drawbacks: the wheels must be driven with exactly the same velocity profile, which can be challenging considering the actual variations between wheels, motors, and environmental differences. It is also difficult for the robot to move on irregular surfaces. Moreover, the orientation of the robot may change abruptly if one active wheel loses contact with the ground [9].

There are two types of nonholonomic constraints governing the motion of the robot platform: Pure rolling constraint and no lateral slip constraint [10]. The pure rolling constraint implies that the robot wheels have a pure rolling motion without any slipping. This constraint is described by the following equations

$$\dot{x}\cos\theta + \dot{y}\sin\theta + L\dot{\theta} = \omega_r R_w, \tag{3}$$

$$\dot{x}\cos\theta + \dot{y}\,sin\,\theta - L\dot{\theta} = \omega_l R_w. \tag{4}$$

The no lateral slip constraint implies that the robot's center point velocity is only in the direction of the axis of symmetry and its lateral component is zero. It is given by

$$\dot{y}\cos\theta - \dot{x}\sin\theta = 0. \tag{5}$$

Without reference to forces and masses, robot kinematics implies a relationship between the position of the robot and its wheels, velocities, and the equations of motion. This section analyzes the mathematical kinematic relationship related to a differentially driven vehicle. The robot configuration is illustrated in **Figure 3**.

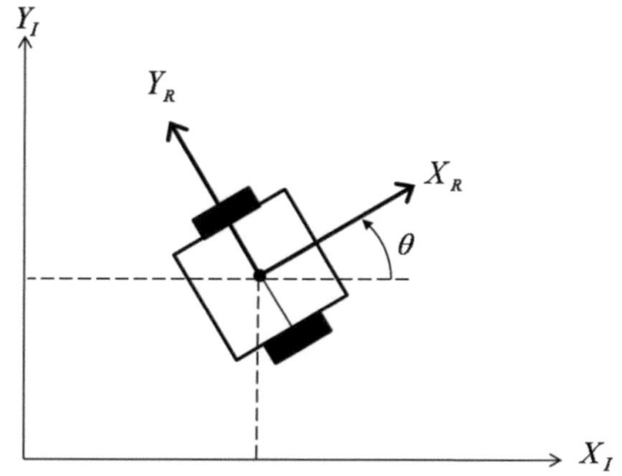

Figure 3. Kinematics of a two-wheel robot.

Let the rotational velocities of the left and right wheel be ω_L and $\omega_{R,}$ respectively, and R_w be the wheel radius then. Then, assuming no wheel slippage, the translational velocities of the wheels are given by

$$v_l = \omega_l R_w, \tag{6}$$

$$v_r = \omega_r R_w. \tag{7}$$

Let the robot forward velocity in the local frame be v, the angular velocity about its Instantaneous Center of Rotation (ICR) axis be ω, and let L be half the distance between the wheels, as shown in **Figure 4**. Then the forward and angular velocities of the robot can be derived from the wheels velocities as follows:

$$\begin{bmatrix} v \\ w \end{bmatrix} = \begin{bmatrix} \frac{1}{2} & \frac{1}{2} \\ \frac{-1}{2L} & \frac{1}{2L} \end{bmatrix} \begin{bmatrix} v_l \\ v_r \end{bmatrix}. \tag{8}$$

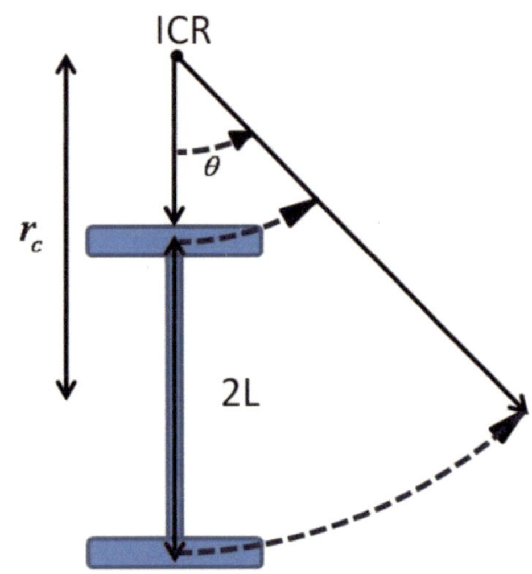

Figure 4. Instantaneous turning radius.

Let θ be the robot orientation with respect to the global x-axis, then the robot velocity vector in the global frame is given by

$$\begin{bmatrix} \dot{x} \\ \dot{y} \\ \dot{\theta} \end{bmatrix} = \begin{bmatrix} \cos\theta & 0 \\ \sin\theta & 0 \\ 0 & 1 \end{bmatrix} \begin{bmatrix} v \\ w \end{bmatrix}. \tag{9}$$

Figure 4 shows the instantaneous turning radius r_c that can be evaluated by

$$r_c = L\left(\frac{v_r + v_l}{v_r - v_l}\right). \tag{10}$$

2.4. Odometry

A robot's global frame position is measured via the dead reckoning method. This method integrates incremental movements measured through wheel encoders and a compass to estimate position, given a known initial start location. The compass delivers the robot's orientation, θ. The incremental movements are measured through wheel encoders and a compass. The robot orientation is θ, while the angular velocities of the left and right wheels ω_l and ω_r, respectively, estimate the two-dimensional position (x, y) via encoders. Encoders utilize encoder pulses to deliver accurate arrival times through the measurement of angular velocities. For encoder resolution, p, and elapsed time, Δt, the angular velocities of the wheels is then defined as

$$\omega_{r,l} = \frac{2\pi}{p\Delta t}. \tag{11}$$

Next, the robot kinematic Eqs (6–9) are used to find the robot velocities $\dot{x}$ and $\dot{y}$. Let T denote a fixed sampling time. Then, the robot position (x, y) in the global frame is found by performing trapezoidal integration

$$x = x_{\text{old}} + \frac{T}{2}(\dot{x} + \dot{x}_{\text{old}}), \tag{12}$$

$$y = y_{\text{old}} + \frac{T}{2}(\dot{y} + \dot{y}_{\text{old}}). \tag{13}$$

Since the position estimation involves a numerical integration of the measurements, there will be an error accumulation over time. As a result, a meaningful estimate of the position cannot be attained with the dead reckoning method.

Systematic and nonsystematic errors are usually encountered with the dead reckoning method. Systematic errors arise due to the misalignment and the unequal diameter of both wheels, while nonsystematic errors may occur as a result of wheel slippage incidents or nonhomogenous environment with uneven floors.

3. Collision avoidance algorithm

In this section, the proposed collision avoidance algorithm is developed using the following parameters. The configuration $q(t_i)$ denotes the position and orientation of the robot in the global frame, while $\mathcal{P}(q(t_i))$ represents only the sensed portion of the environment. This measured portion of the environment is used to construct the robot's workspace polar map, which allows the set of obstacles $\mathcal{O}(q(t_i))$ to be identified and the configuration space $\mathcal{C}$ to be computed. Next, the operation of the robot is performed in the C-space to simplify the motion planning and navigation. The motion of the two-dimensional robot in the global frame can be simplified to that of a one point (robot reference point) in the C-space. The optimum steering angle γ_{desired} is selected by identifying all the workspace obstacles and classifying the available gaps that can be accessed by the robot. The nonholonomic constraints are taken into account by computing the required radius of curvature r_c such that $Q_{t_i,T}$ which is the set of configurations of the trajectory followed from $q(t_i)$ to $q(t_i + T)$ does not intersect with any obstacle, $\mathcal{A}(Q_{t_i,T}) \bigcap \mathcal{O}(q(t_i)) = \emptyset$. This is achieved by restricting the radius of curvature to an adaptive upper bound. Finally, the robot executes the control action $u_i = (\gamma_{\text{desired}}, r_c)$. The process is repeated until the robot converges to the target position q_{target}. The algorithm is pictorially illustrated in **Figure 5**.

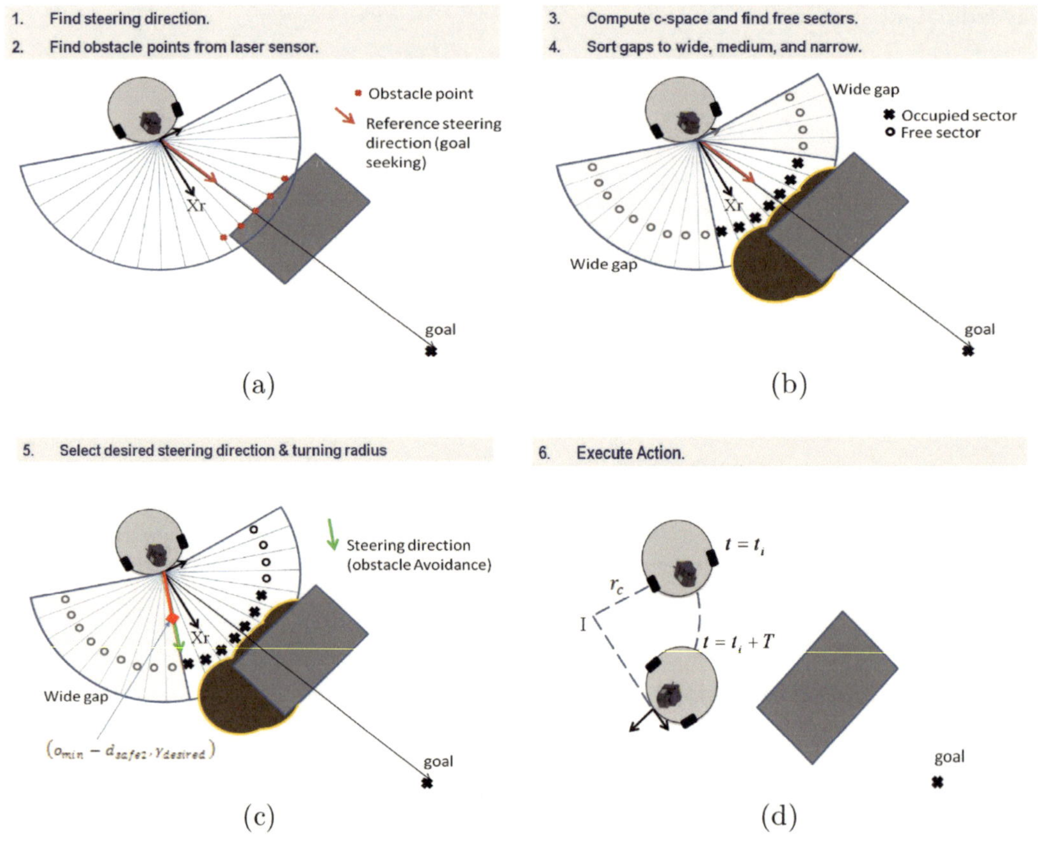

Figure 5. Reactive navigation algorithm in action.

3.1. Identification of reference steering angle

The steering angle with which the robot takes in the absence of obstacles is referred to as the reference steering angle, γ_{ref}. It is an intermediate variable that will later help us find the desired steering angle γ_{desired}, which is derived as follows. Let the robot configuration shown in **Figure 6** be:

$$q_r = (x_r, y_r, \theta_r), \tag{14}$$

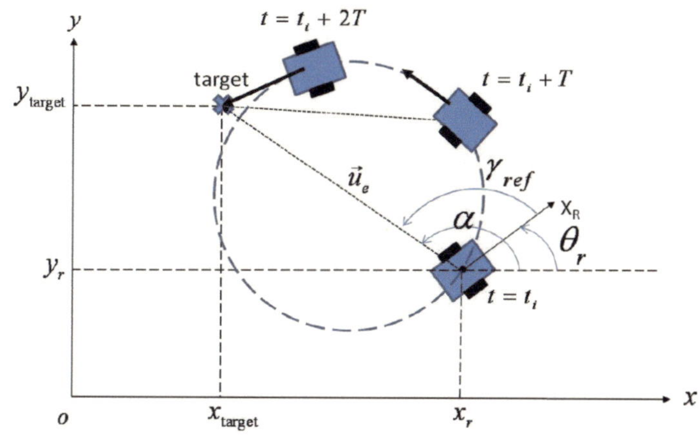

Figure 6. The robot's trajectory to q_{target} in the absence of obstacles.

where (x_r, y_r) is the position of the robot in the $x - y$ plane, and $\theta_r \in [0, 2\pi)$ is the robot's orientation with respect to the x-axis.

Let the target configuration be

$$q_{\text{target}} = (x_{\text{target}}, y_{\text{target}}, \theta_{\text{target}}). \tag{15}$$

Let $\vec{u}_e$ be the vector connecting the robot reference point to the target location. The phase angle of $\vec{u}_e$ is given by

$$\alpha = \arctan\frac{y_{\text{target}} - y_r}{x_{\text{target}} - x_r}. \tag{16}$$

Orientation error is corrected for by turning the robot in an angle defined as follows: $\gamma_{ref} = \alpha - \theta_r, -\pi \le \gamma_{ref} \le \pi$. The range of γ_{ref} is chosen in such a way that the smaller turning angle is selected. The robot can turn clockwise (right) or counter clockwise (left). **Figure 6** illustrates the trajectory taken by the robot to move to the target configuration. The robot finally achieves a straight line path once its x-axis is on line with the error vector.

3.2. Model of robot environment

The robot environment is modeled by constructing a polar map of the workspace in the local robot frame. At a given instant of time, the distances from the robot to all the surrounding obstacles are measured by a laser range finder and used to build the partial polar map. The laser range sensor is calibrated to scan the 200° front view of the robot in 20 sectors with a 10° angular resolution, as illustrated in **Figure 7**. The measured data is returned as a set of data points:

$$\mathcal{P}(q(t_i)) = \{p_1, p_2, \ldots, p_j, \ldots, p_{20}\}. \tag{17}$$

A point p_j is expressed by a pair (d_j, β_j) where d_j is the distance between the robot and the obstacle at sector j. β_j is the orientation of the jth sector, S_j, with respect to the local x-axis. The subset of workspace obstacles seen at configuration $q(t_i)$ is identified by applying a threshold on d_j,

$$\mathcal{O}(q(t_i)) = \{p_j \in \mathcal{P}(q(t_i)) \mid d_j \le R_{safe}\}. \tag{18}$$

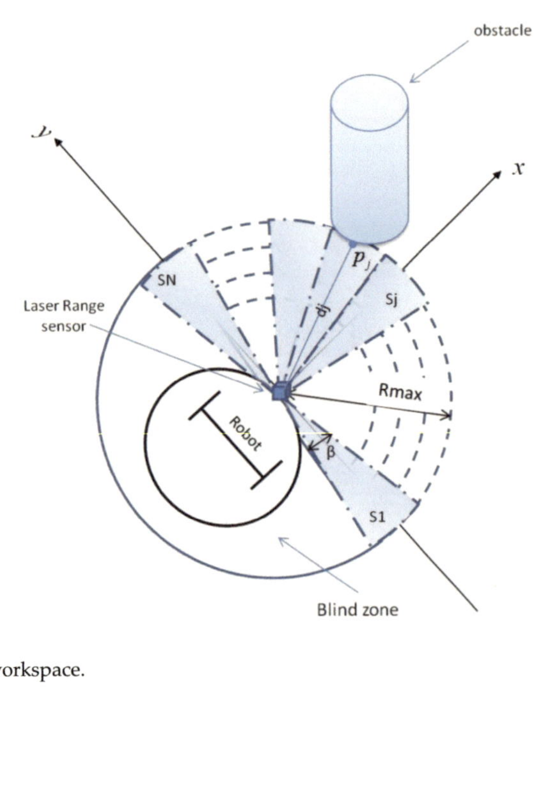

Figure 7. Polar map of the workspace.

The choice of the threshold R_{safe} plays an important role in the obstacle avoidance algorithm. If R_{safe} is large, then the obstacle avoidance will start too soon which results in a suboptimal path. Also, by selecting a large R_{safe}, the algorithm may fail to detect any gaps in the environment and, therefore, incorrectly report a trap situation. For example, the robot in **Figure 8** successfully detects a gap in the environment with R_{safe1} but fails to do so when using a large value R_{safe2}.

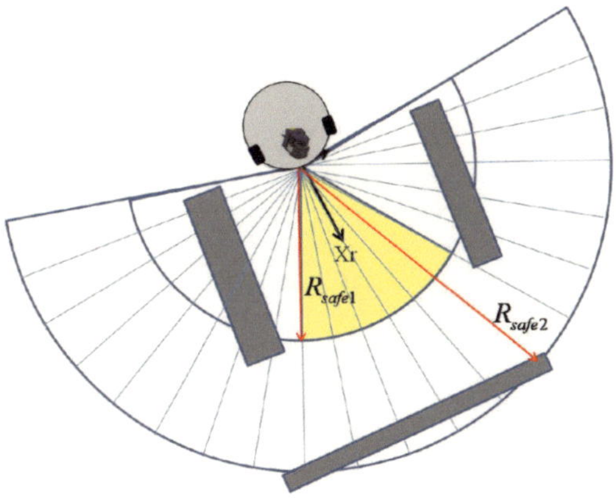

Figure 8. The effect of using a large value for R_{safe}.

The detection range threshold R_{safe} is allowed to take different values depending on the situation encountered:

$$R_{safe} = \begin{cases} 0.1\,m & \text{if robot is close to target configuration;} \\ 0.5\,m & \text{otherwise.} \end{cases} \tag{19}$$

The robot is considered close to the target configuration if:

$$(x_{target} - x_r)^2 + (y_{target} - y_r)^2 \le \varepsilon \tag{20}$$

where ε is the target threshold.

3.3. Evaluation of configuration space

The 2D robot with radius R computes the C_{obst} for a given set of workspace obstacles, $\mathcal{O}$. Assume for a moment that a single obstacle exists, $\mathcal{O} = \{p_j\}$. As illustrated in **Figure 9**, $\mathcal{C}_{obst}$ is found through tracing the robot's configuration as it slides around p_j. Hence, the following relations can be written for Circle C_j enclosing $\mathcal{C}_{obst}$ with Radius R and center $I_j = (I_{j,x}, I_{j,y})$:

$$\mathcal{C}_{\text{obst}} = \{q \in \mathcal{C} \mid (x - I_{j,x})^2 + (y - I_{j,y})^2 \le R^2\}, \tag{21}$$

$$I_{j,x} = R + d_j \cos\beta_j, \tag{22}$$

$$I_{j,y} = d_j \sin\beta_j, -100^\circ \le \beta_j \le 100^\circ. \tag{23}$$

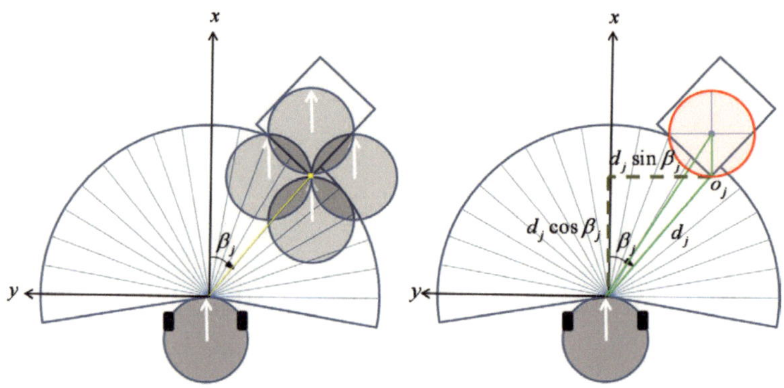

Figure 9. C-space algorithm.

Next, we find the radial distance L_i which is the radial distance between the robot and the boundary of $\mathcal{C}_j$ at angle β_i. The equation of C_j in polar coordinates is

$$\rho_j = \sqrt{I_{j,x}^2 + I_{j,y}^2}, \qquad \phi_j = atan2(\frac{I_{j,y}}{I_{j,x}}), \tag{24}$$

$$L_i^2 + \rho_j^2 - 2\rho_j L_i \cos(\beta_i - \phi_j) = R^2. \tag{25}$$

Equation 24 can be solved for L_i, giving:

$$L_i = \min\{\rho_j \cos(\beta_i - \phi_j) \pm \sqrt{R^2 - \rho_j^2 \sin^2(\beta_i - \phi_j)}\}, \qquad \alpha_{\min} \le \beta_i \le \alpha_{\max}. \tag{26}$$

Equation 26 has a real value if $\alpha_{\min}$ and $\alpha_{\max}$ are selected as:

$$\alpha_{\min} = \min\{\phi_j \pm \sin\frac{R}{\rho_j}\}, \qquad \alpha_{\max} = \max\{\phi_j \pm \sin\frac{R}{\rho_j}\} \tag{27}$$

The above analysis is for the case when $\mathcal{O}$ contains a single obstacle point. In the common case where $\mathcal{O}$ consists of m obstacle points, C_{obst} is found by:

$$\mathcal{C}_{obst} = \bigcup_{1 \le j \le m} \mathcal{C}_j. \tag{28}$$

The exact robots radius was utilized to enlarge the obstacle points. However, control errors arise within the algorithm even when using accurate robot dimensions. Therefore, the radius is modified to $R_s = R + d_{\text{safe}}$. This serves as a space buffer that adds a safety margin. In our implementation d_{safe} is chosen to be 20% of the robot radius.

3.4. Selection of desired steering angle

The sectors in $\mathcal{C}$ are classified as free or occupied. The jth sector S_j is occupied if $L_j \le R_{\text{safe}}$; otherwise, it is free. Adjacent free sectors are grouped together to form gaps. Let N_{free} denote the number of sectors forming a gap. The gaps are classified as follows:

$$gap = \begin{cases} wide & \text{if } N_{\text{free}} > 3, \\ medium & \text{if } N_{\text{free}} = 3, \\ narrow & \text{if } N_{\text{free}} < 3. \end{cases} \tag{29}$$

The desired steering angle is set as the angle of the gap edge with minimum cost. To ensure the selection of the widest possible gap, the search at the beginning is performed over the free wide gaps. if no solution exists within this category, the algorithm searches for a gap in the medium category. The algorithm searches within the narrow gaps, only if the latter two categories did not contain any solution.

$$\text{Cost}(\beta_j) = c_1(\gamma_{\text{ref}} - \beta_j) + c_2\beta_j. \tag{30}$$

The equation is explained as follows: the term $c_1(\gamma_{\text{ref}} - \beta_j)$ refers to the closeness of the goal location to the desired steering direction. The second term, $c_2\beta_j$, indicates how close the current robot heading is to the current steering direction. The coefficients are chose to be $c_1 = 0.3$ and $c_2 = 0.7$, as with this, more weight is given to the steering angles resulting in a smoother trajectory.

In **Figure 10**, the oscillatory trajectory of the robot is exemplified. At the initial start time t_0, the robot's polar map has gaps G_1 and G_2. At this time, the robots steers toward G_2 as it closer to the q_{target}. After an elapsed time T, the robot no longer has G_2 within its range as it achieves a better view, steering the robot toward G_1. However, this action brings the robots back to its initial state at t_0 where both gaps are visible. With this repetitive motion, the robot gets trapped in an infinite loop of repetitive actions. One way to solve this problem is to adjust the steering angle adaptively and smooth the trajectory while avoiding the trap situations as described later in the chapter.

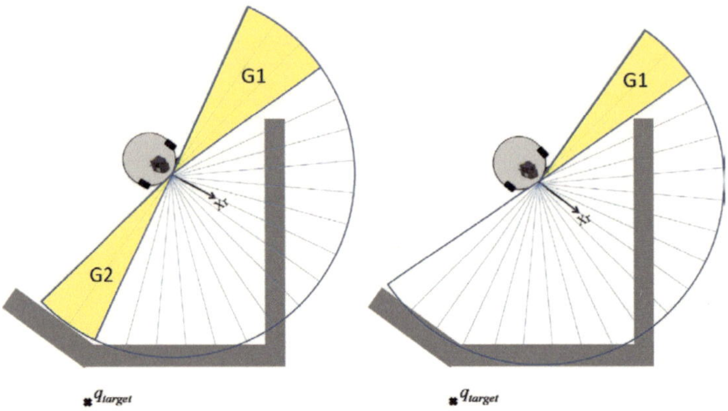

Figure 10. Trajectory oscillation scenario due to a trapped situation.

The algorithm used to select the desired steering angle is summarized as follows:

if $\gamma_{\text{ref}} \in \mathcal{G}$ **then**

$$\gamma_{\text{desired}} = \gamma_{\text{ref}}$$

elseif $\mathcal{G}_{\text{wide}} \neq \phi$ **then**

$$\gamma_{\text{desired}} = \arg \min_{\beta_j \in \mathcal{G}_{\text{wide}}} Cost(\beta_j).$$

else if $\mathcal{G}_{\text{medium}} \neq \phi$ **then**

$$\gamma_{\text{desired}} = \arg \min_{\beta_j \in \mathcal{G}_{\text{medium}}} Cost(\beta_j).$$

else if $\mathcal{G}_{\text{narrow}} \neq \phi$ **then**

$$\gamma_{\text{desired}} = \arg \min_{\beta_j \in \mathcal{G}_{\text{narrow}}} Cost(\beta_j).$$

else

Turn 180° around.

end if

end if

3.5. Identification of adaptive radius of curvature

The robot follows a circular arc with constant wheel velocities instead of the desired steering angle due to the nonholonomic kinematic constraint. A collision could take place when going from the initial to the final path configuration as it may be interested with $\mathcal{C}_{obst}(q(t_i))$. An example of a collision is demonstrated in **Figure 11**, where the robot had steered with a relatively large radius.

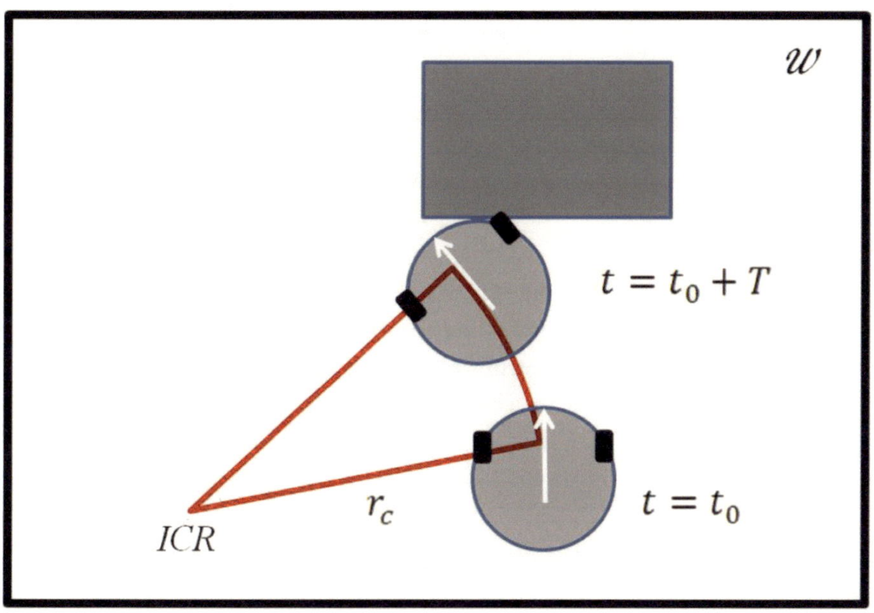

Figure 11. The robot collides with an obstacle because it uses a large turning radius.

The sector along the local x-axis is labeled as S_0 and the sector along the desired steering angle is labeled as S_{desired}. Next, define L_j^m as the distance between the robot front reference point and the obstacle point o_j as shown in **Figure 12**. This distance is evaluated in terms of the variable L_j as follows:

$$L_j^m = \sqrt{(L_j \cos\beta_j + a)^2 + (L_j \sin\beta_j)^2}, \tag{35}$$

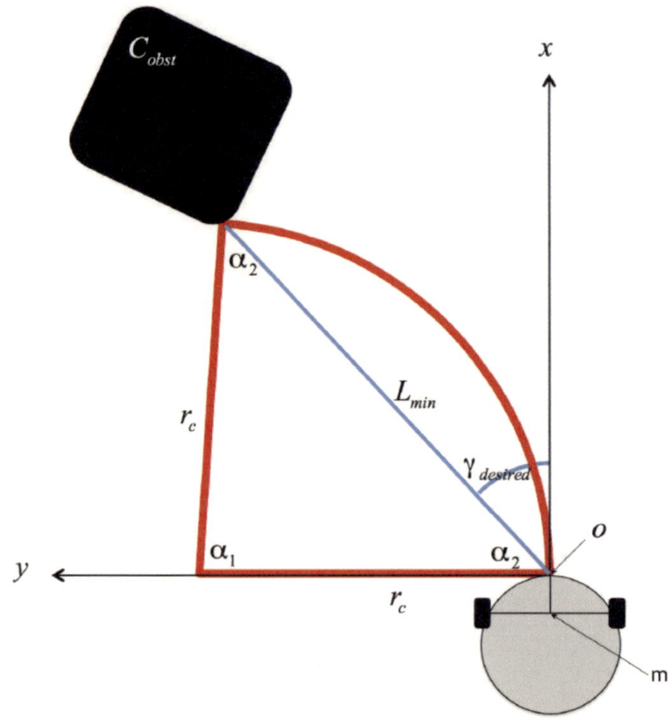

Figure 12. Turning radius selection.

where a is the actual distance separating the middle point m of the wheels axis from the robot front reference point. $L_{\min}$ is then defined as the minimum distance to the nearest obstacle point situated between S_{desired} and S_0. The optimum turning radius r_c is selected so that the robot trajectory goes through ($L_{\min}$, γ_{desired}) as shown in **Figure 12**. The turning radius is derived as follows. Consider the isosceles triangle where the two equal sides have length r_c and the remaining side has length $L_{\min}$. From the law of cosines,

$$L_{\min}^2 = 2r_c^2 - 2r_c^2 \cos\alpha_1. \tag{36}$$

α_1 can be found as

$$\alpha_1 + 2\alpha_2 = 180, \tag{37}$$

$$\alpha_2 = 90 - \gamma_{\text{desired}}, \tag{38}$$

$$\Rightarrow \alpha_1 = 2\gamma_{\text{desired}}. \tag{39}$$

http://dx.doi.org/10.5772/64227

Using the double angle formula and equation 32, we can find r_c as

$$r_c = \frac{L_{\min}}{2\sin(\gamma_{\text{desired}})}. \tag{40}$$

A safety margin is introduced by reducing the turning radius so that the robot passes through the point ($L_{\min} - d_{\text{safe2}}$, γ_{desired}) instead. Also, the turning radius r_c is forced to saturate if it is greater than a threshold value r_{large}. In our implementation, d_{safe2} is selected to be 1.2R and $r_{\text{large}} = 0.5$m.

4. Experimental results

4.1. Mobile robot platform

A prototype robot platform was designed and built to validate the proposed algorithms. The platform has a differential drive mechanism and is designed to operate indoors on flat solid surfaces. Forward, backward, and steered motion is generated by controlling the right and left wheel velocities based on the differential steering concept. The platform control system includes a single board computer and a microcontroller, thus providing a dependable and strong computing environment. The platform comprises also a large range of sensors including ultrasonic sensors and a laser range sensor for obstacle detection, as well as a compass and encoders for localization. **Figure 13** shows a front view picture of the mobile robot platform.

The obstacle avoidance algorithms described earlier are tested on the mobile robot platform in different environment settings. The testing is conducted indoors in a lab environment where the lab furniture is to be avoided. The obstacles are arranged in five different scenarios that vary in difficulty. For all scenarios, the sample time is $T = 1$ s, the robot initial configuration is (0, 0, − 90°) while the target x–y location is (1.6 m, − 1.5 m). Hence, the initial error in position is 2.1932 m.

4.2. Environment setting 1

The robot's initial configuration is connected to the target configuration through a direct path indicated by a straight line as observed in **Figure 14a**. The trajectory, of length 2.2711 m, is depicted in **Figure 14b**. In **Figure 14c**, the robot's velocities are presented and are smooth in the global frame. **Figure 14d** exemplifies the control action. An infinite radius of 0.5 is set for keeping the plot in rage as the robot would steer in an infinite radius when moving in a straight line.

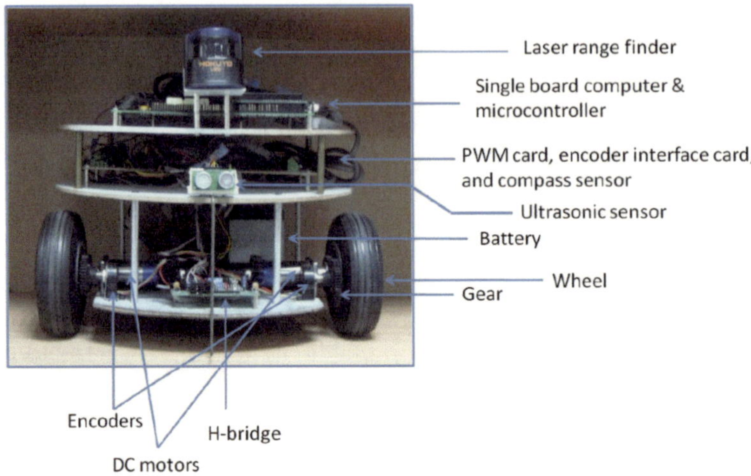

Figure 13. Mobile robot platform.

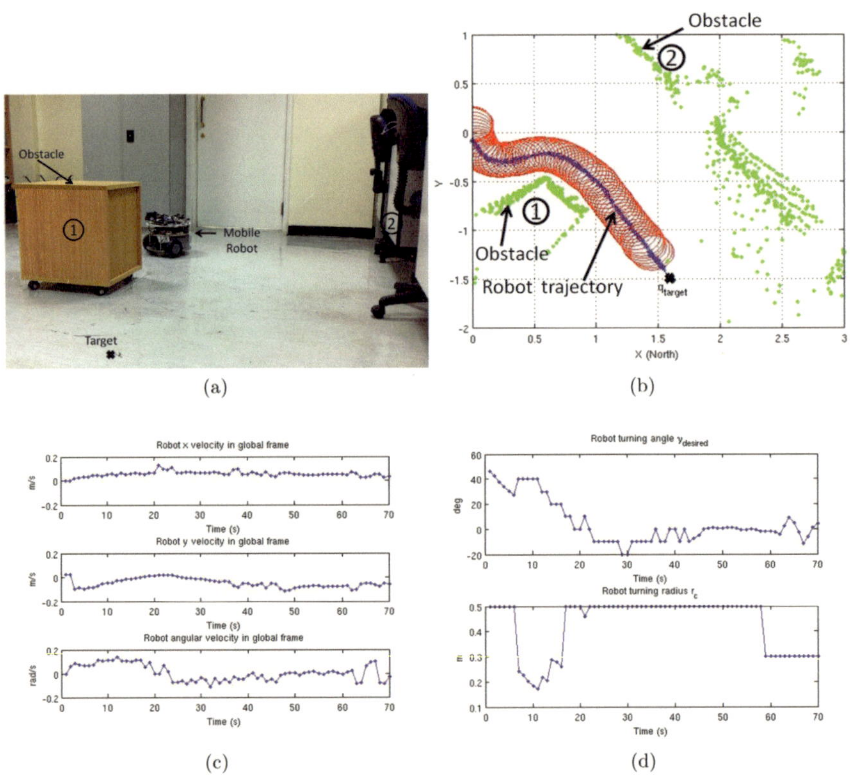

Figure 14. Experimental results. (a) Robot initial position, target position, and the surrounding obstacles; (b) The obstacle points in green, the area occupied by the robot at each instance in time in red, and the reference point trajectory in blue; (c) The robot velocities; (d) The robot control action.

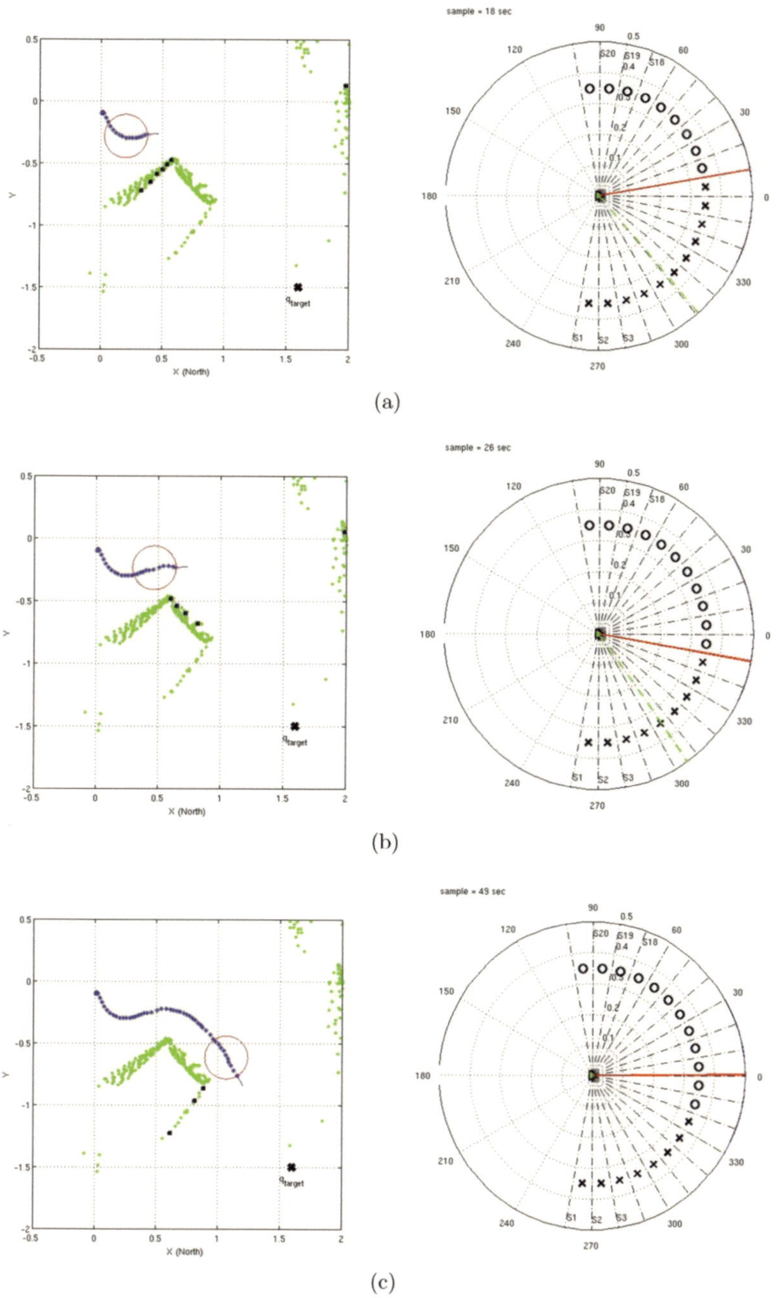

Figure 15. Illustration of the trajectory control algorithm at different time intervals. The obstacles surrounding the robot at a given instant of time are shown as black dots in the Cartesian coordinate frame. A rough estimate of the obstacle contour is defined by the solid yellow line. The classified sectors are shown in the polar histogram. The desired steering angle is indicated by a dashed green line, while the reference steering angle is indicated by a solid red line.

Critical time samples with some intermediate values are shown in **Figure 15**. At a sample of 12 s, the robot is only capable of viewing the square obstacles front side. This classifies the front gaps as occupied. The reference steering angle is classified to be in an occupied sector as it is of −20° value. Hence, the reference angle $\gamma_{desired}$ with a value 30° is selected as the next best alternative, and the corresponding turning radius is approximately 0.205 m as shown in **Figure 14d**. **Figure 15b** illustrates the robot at a sample time of 26 s. At this sample, the robot can only observe the obstacles' right side and has a γ_{ref} of −54° and a $\gamma_{desired}$ of −10°. Additionally, the robot takes a turn with a 0.5 m radius. The sample at 49 s is seen in **Figure 15c**. $\gamma_{desired}$ is simply equated to γ_{ref} as it resides in a free sector. This moves the robot straight to the target. This scenario course was completed within 70 s.

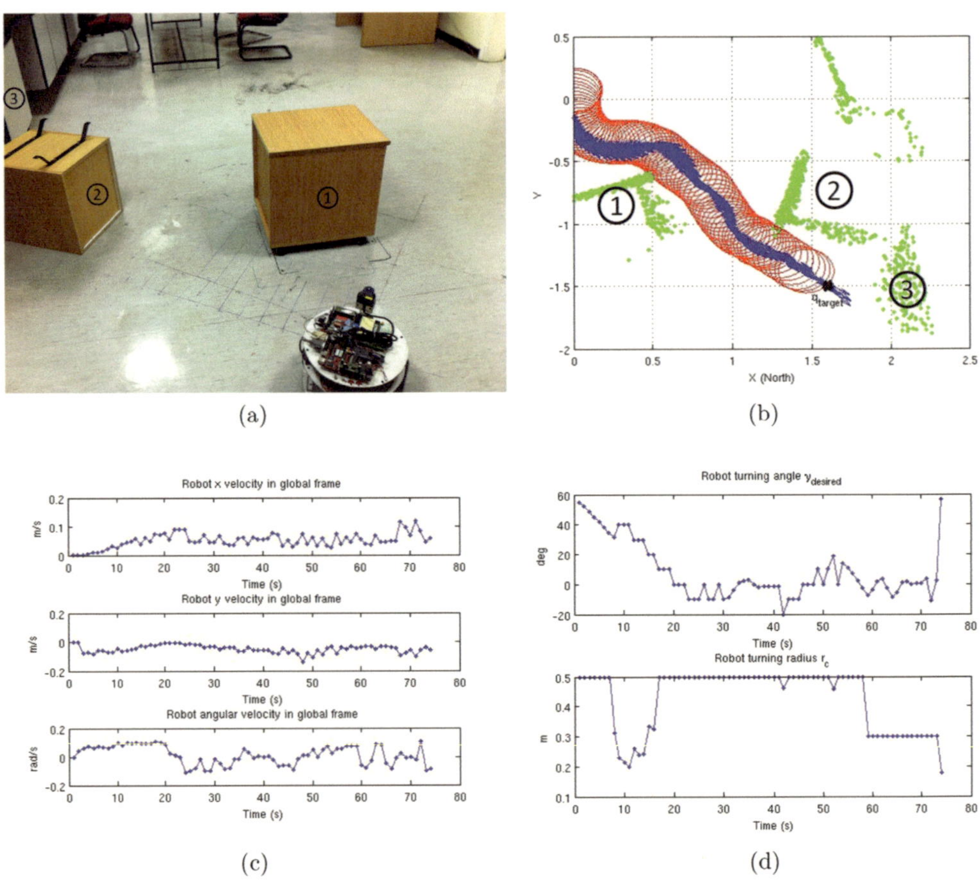

Figure 16. Experiment 2 results. (a) The robot initial position, target position, and the surrounding obstacles; (b) The obstacle points in green, the area occupied by the robot at each instance in time in red, and the reference point trajectory in blue. (c) The robot velocities; (d) The robot control vector.

http://dx.doi.org/10.5772/64227

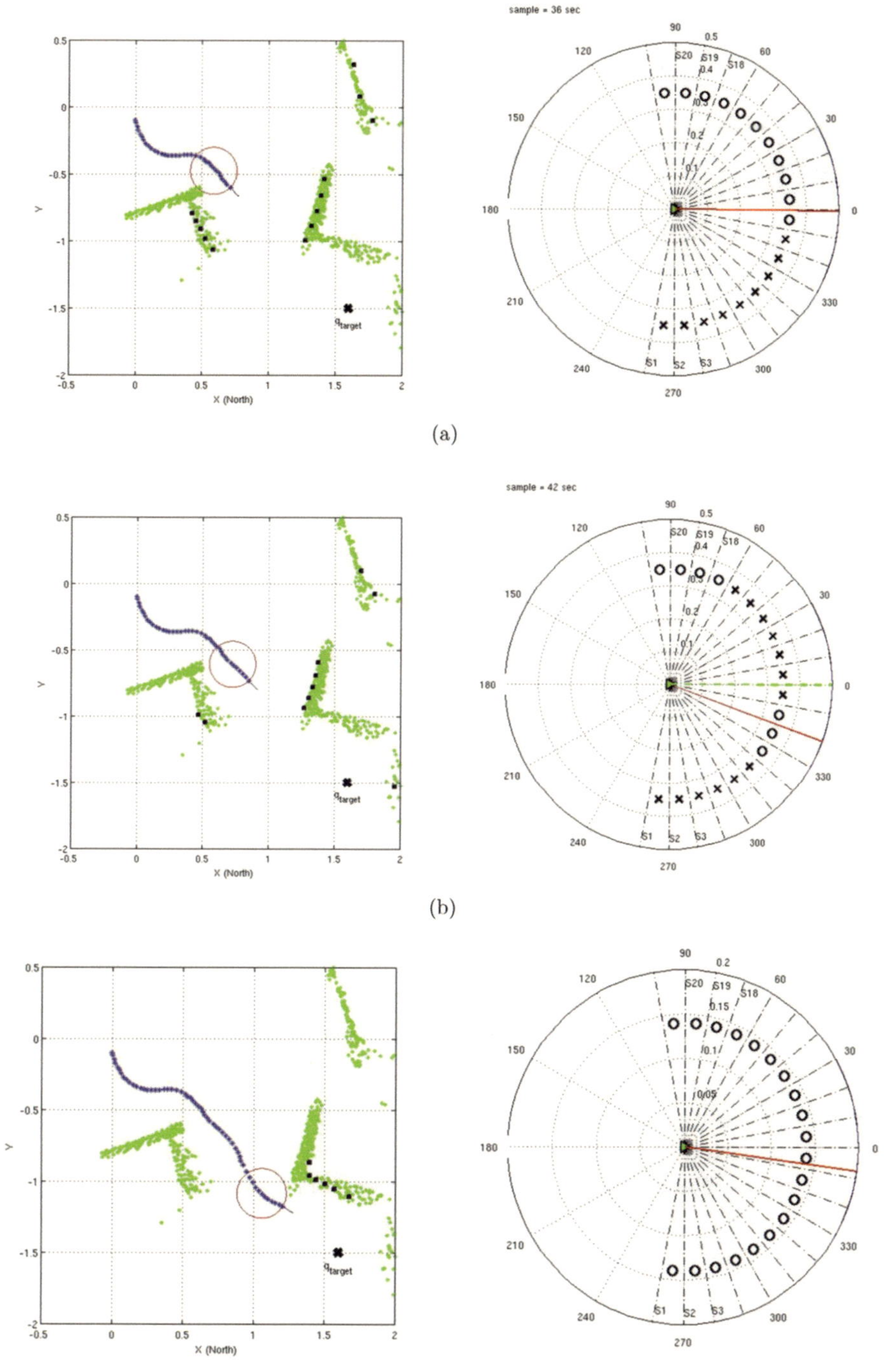

Figure 17. (a) Shows the robot entering the passage; (b) shows the robot inside the passage; (c) shows the robot exiting the passage.

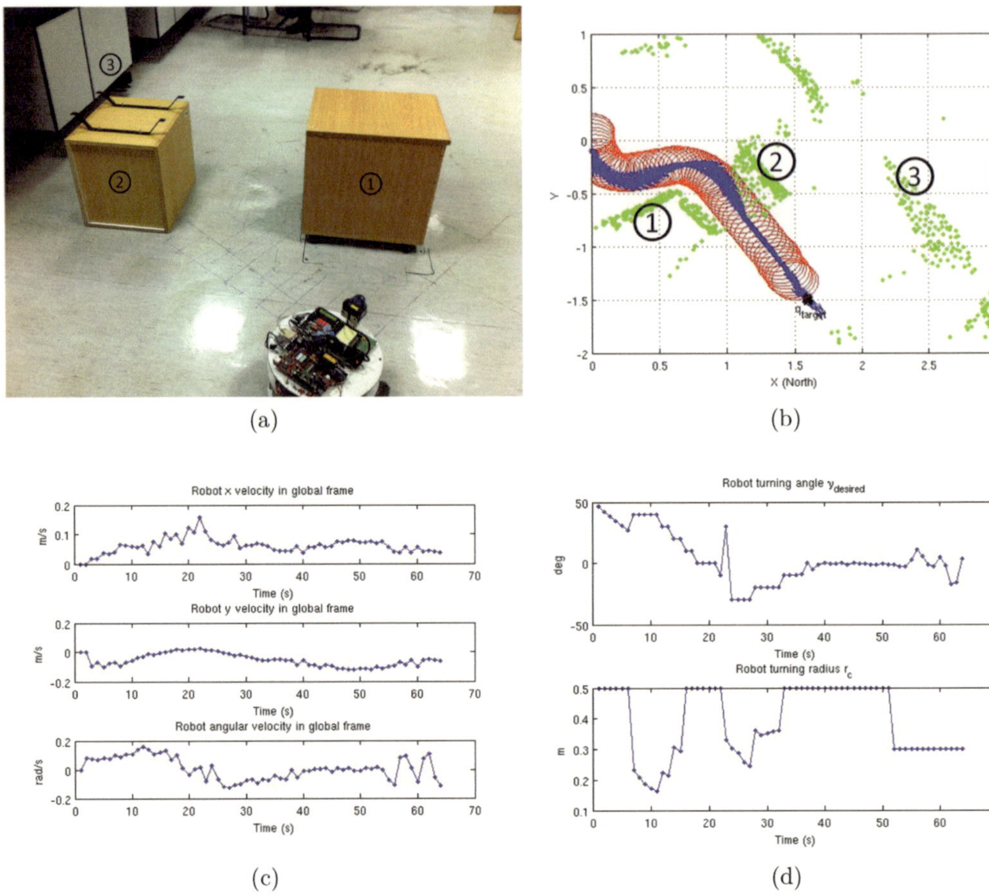

Figure 18. Experiment 3 results. (a) The robot testing environment; (b) the robot trajectory; (c) the robot velocities; (d) the robot control vector.

4.3. Environment setting 2

A scenario of wide entrance but narrow exit was modeled as in **Figure 16a**. The robot was able to make it through the passage within 74 s and with a 2.2539 m trajectory length, shown in **Figure 16b** below. Figue 16c and 16d depict the robot velocities and control actions, respectively. **Figure 17** illustrates with polar histograms for when the robot first enters the passageway, moves within it and then exits.

4.4. Environment setting 3

The difference in this scenario is that the narrow nature of the passage way is greater than that depicted in scenario 2, as shown in **Figure 18a**. As a result, the robots ability to pick up on and detect the narrow gaps that are only slightly larger than its size is tested. As shown in **Figure 18b**, the robot successfully makes it through the pathway and its corresponding

http://dx.doi.org/10.5772/64227

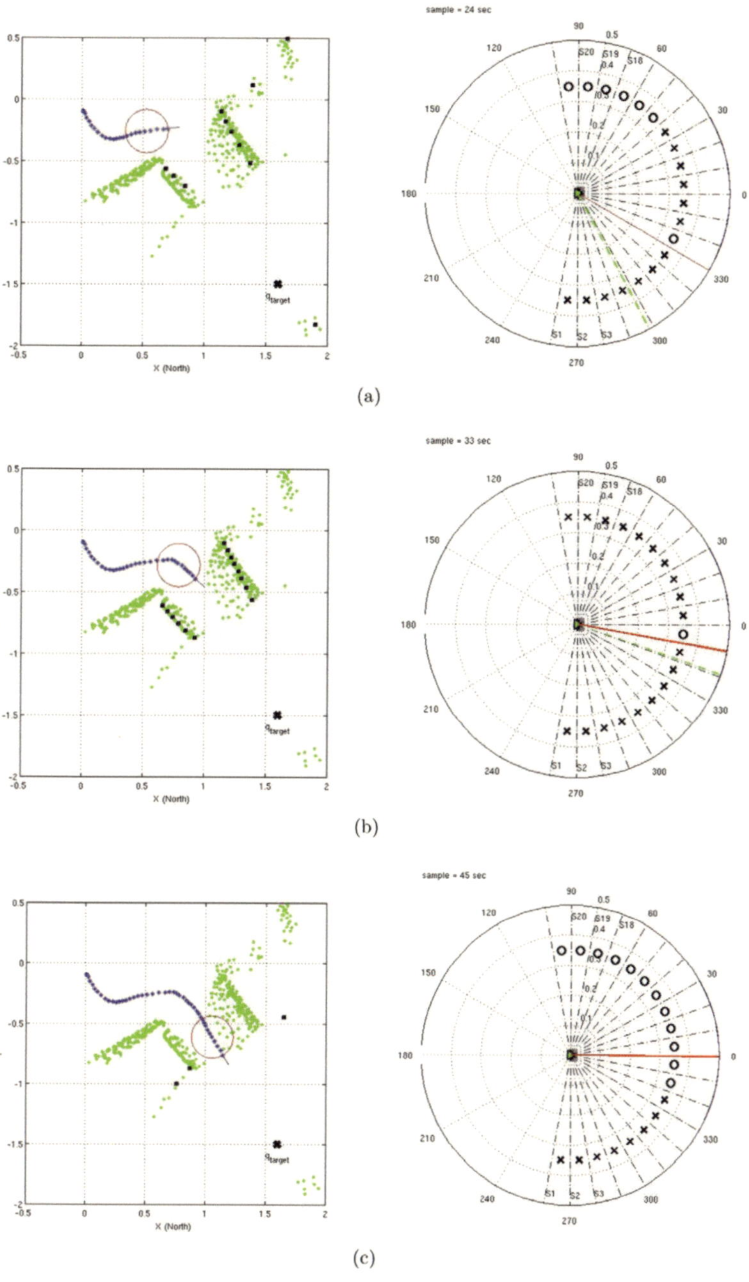

Figure 19. (a) Shows the robot entering the passage; (b) Shows the robot inside the passage; (c) Shows the robot exiting the passage.

velocities and control actions during the trajectory are illustrated in **Figure 18c** and **18d**, respectively. **Figure 19** provides details via histograms from when the robot enters to when it leaves the passageway 19.

4.5. Environment setting 4

The difference between this scenario, depicted in **Figure 20a**, and scenario 3 is the addition of an obstacle to block the exit from the passageway, forming a dead end for the robot. The trajectory taken by the robot is presented in **Figure 20b**, **20c**, and **20d** represent the robot's velocity and control actions through this passageway, respectively. In **Figure 20c**, fluctuations left and right can be seen for the turning angle, γ_{desired}. However, at $t = 31$ s the robot approaches the dead end and comes to realize that the narrow gap is in fact blocked. The robot thus steers left and now envisions the dead end as a gap, resulting in the robots attempt to steer toward it once more. This is illustrated in **Figure 21c**. After 179 s, the robot completes the mission of contouring the obstacles and overcoming the oscillations back and forth having travelled a total of 6.0243 m.

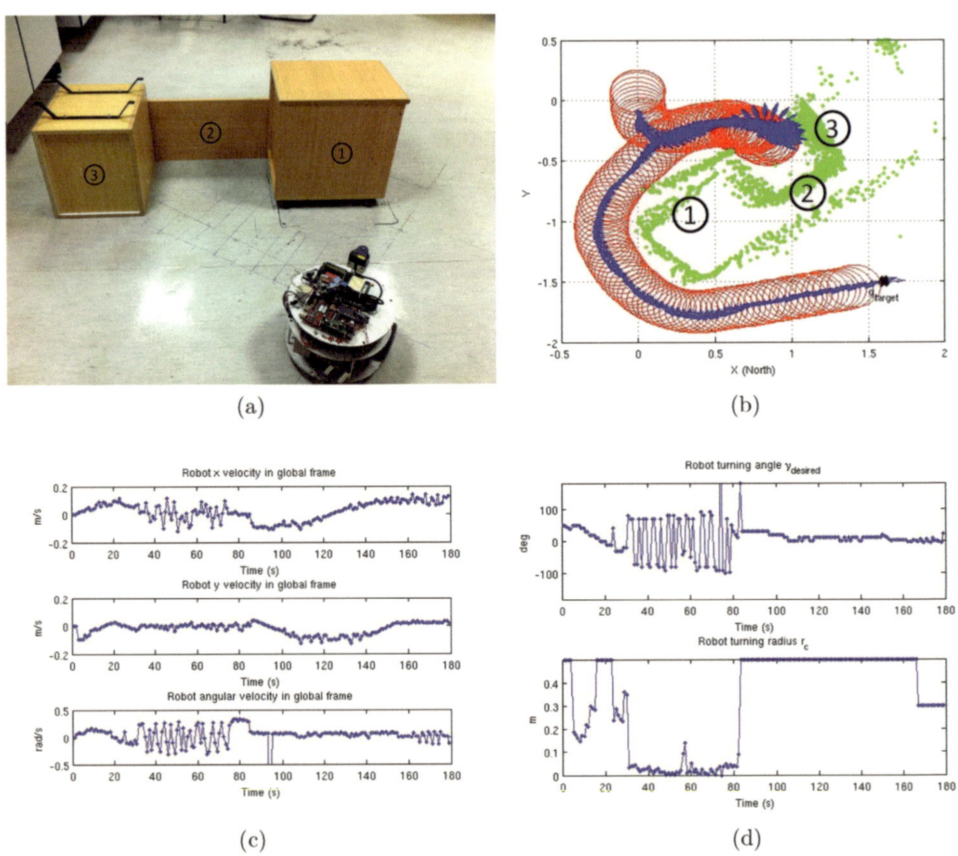

Figure 20. Experiment 4 results (a) The robot initial position, target position, and the surrounding obstacles; (b) The obstacle points in green, the area occupied by the robot at each instance in time in red, and the reference point trajectory in blue; (c) The robot velocities; (d) The robot control vector.

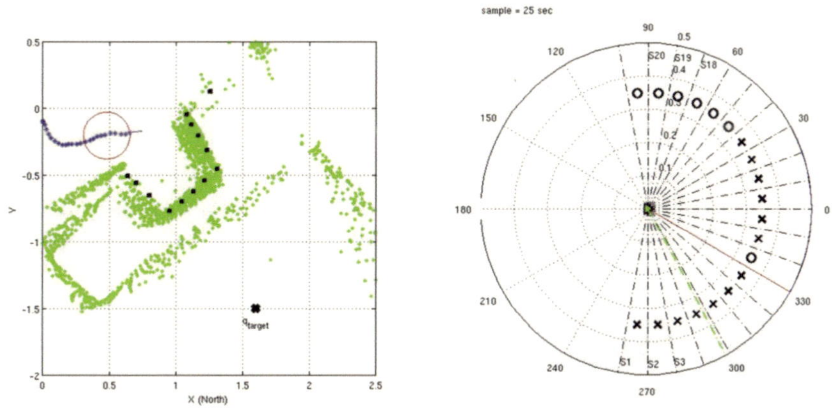

(a)

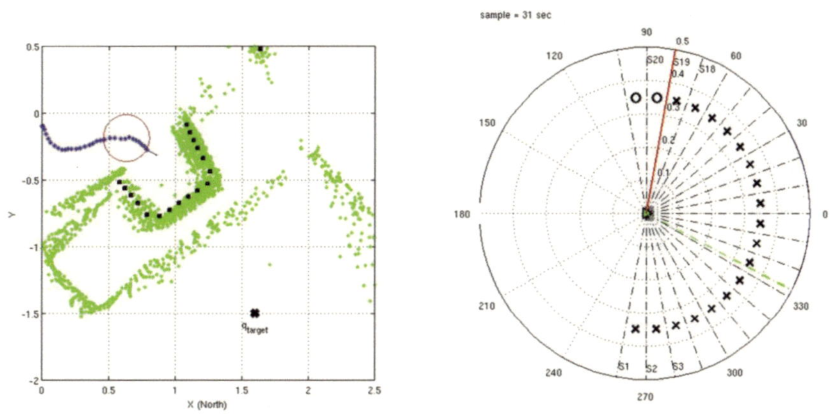

(b)

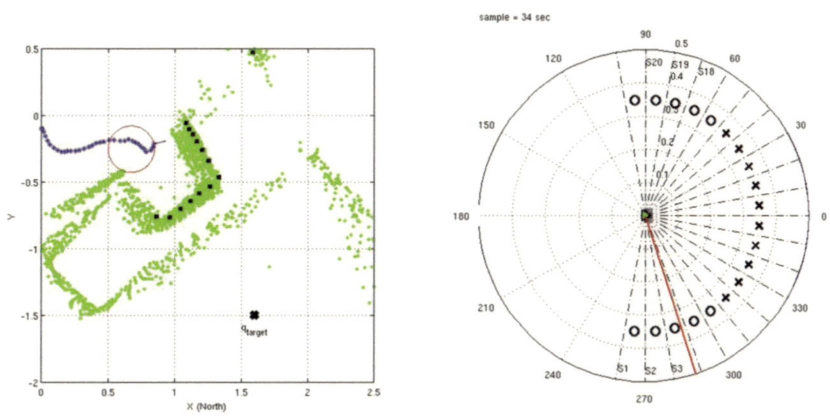

(c)

Figure 21. (a) Robot detects a passage; (b) robot discovers a dead end and attempt to turn away; (c) after the robot moves away, the dead end appears as a gap.

4.6. Environment setting 5

The three obstacles in scenario 5 are placed in such a way to form a narrow gap that is smaller than the robot size. This makes the robot's initial steering to fall into a blocked path as depicted in **Figure 22a**. The robot ends up at the target location due to its nature to persistently search for a gap, as illustrated in **Figure 22b**, the target location as shown in **Figure 22b**. The robot velocities and control actions are depicted in **Figure 22c** and **Figure 22d**, once more, depict the robot's respective velocities and control actions.

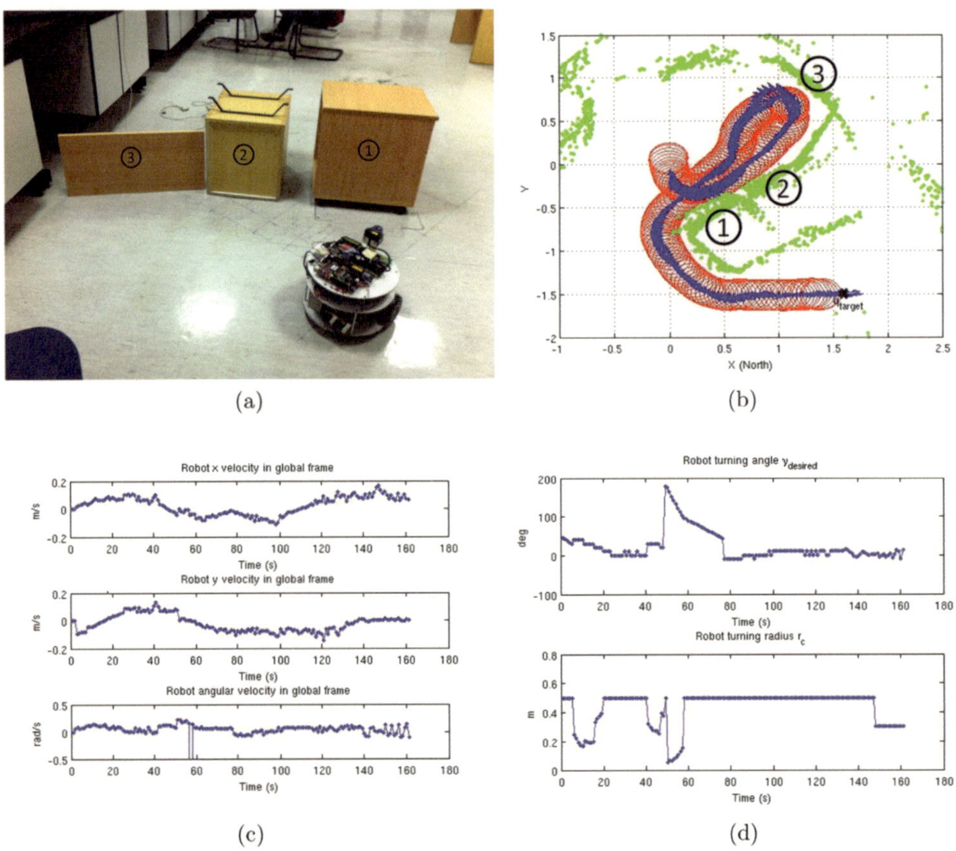

Figure 22. Experiment 5 results. (a) The robot testing environment; (b) The robot trajectory; (c) The robot velocities; (d) The robot control vector.

5. Conclusion

This chapter presents a reactive navigation algorithm for a wheeled mobile robot under nonholonomic constraints and in unknown environments. The mobile robot can travel safely and efficiently to a preset destination having no prior knowledge of the environment. The shape and dimensions of the robot are all incorporated to produce the control algorithm that determines the set of all steering angles that result in no collisions. The selection of the steering angle depends on the one that is closest to the target and is identified as the widest gap. In addition, the algorithm takes into account the nonholonomic constraints of differentially steered robots by computing circular trajectories with adaptive radius of curvature. A mobile robot platform was built and used to assess and validate the performance of the algorithms over a variety of unstructured indoor environments. The results demonstrate that the navigation algorithm is capable of driving the robot safely through different obstacle arrangements and avoids successfully trap situations.

Author details

Mariam Al-Sagban* and Rached Dhaouadi

*Address all correspondence to: g00006931@aus.edu

American University of Sharjah, Sharjah, the United Arab Emirates

References

[1] M. Al-Sagban, "Autonomous robot navigation based on recurrent neural networks," Master's thesis, American University of Sharjah, 2012.

[2] *Robots attempt record breaking Pacific Ocean voyage*. http://www.bbc.co.uk/news/technology-15790088, 14, March 2012.

[3] *Honda shows smarter robot, helps in nuclear crisis*. http://www.taiwannews.com.tw/etn/news_content.php?id=1753308, 09, Nov 2011.

[4] R. Siegwart and I. R. Nourbakhsh, *Introduction to Autonomous Mobile Robots*. Scituate, MA, USA: Bradford Company, 2004.

[5] M. AlSagban and R. Dhaouadi, "Neural-based navigation of a differential-drive mobile robot," in *12th International Conference on Control Automation Robotics & Vision (ICARCV)*, 2012, pp. 353–358.

[6] W.H. Mark Spong and M. Vidyasagar, *Robot Modeling and Control*. New York, USA: Wiley, 2006.

[7] M.V. Mark W. Spong, Seth Hutchinson, *Principles of robot motion: Theory, algorithms, and implementation*. Cambridge, Mass. [u.a.]: MIT Press, 2005.

[8] J. Minguez, F. Lamiraux, and J.-P. Laumond, "Motion planning and obstacle avoidance," in *Springer Handbook of Robotics*, B. Siciliano and O. Khatib, Eds. Springer Berlin

Heidelberg, 2008, pp. 827–852, 10.1007/978-3-540-30301-5_36. [Online]. Available: http://dx.doi.org/10.1007/978-3-540-30301-5_36

[9] G. Campion and W. Chung, "Wheeled robots," in *Springer Handbook of Robotics*, B. Siciliano and O. Khatib, Eds. Springer Berlin Heidelberg, 2008, pp. 391–410, 10.1007/978-3-540-30301-5_18. [Online]. Available: http://dx.doi.org/10.1007/978-3-540-30301-5_18

[10] O. Mohareri and R. Dhaouadi, "A neural network based adaptive tracking controller for nonholonomic wheeled mobile robots with unknown dynamics," in *Proc. of the ASME 2010 International Mechanical Engineering Congress & Exposition (IMECE2010)*, vol. 6, November 12–18, 2010.

Chapter 4

Occupancy Map Construction for Indoor Robot Navigation

Dora-Luz Almanza-Ojeda, Yazmín Gomar-Vera and
Mario-Alberto Ibarra-Manzano

Additional information is available at the end of the chapter

http://dx.doi.org/10.5772/64871

Abstract

Robot mobile navigation is a hard task that requires, essentially, avoiding static and dynamic objects. This chapter presents a strategy for constructing an occupancy map by proposing a probabilistic model of an ultrasonic sensor, during robot indoor navigation. A local map is initially constructed using the ultrasonic sensor mounted in the front of the robot. This map provides the position of the nearest obstacles in the scene useful for achieving the reactive navigation. The encoders allow computing the robot location in the initial local map. A first path for robot navigation based on the initial local map is estimated using the potential field strategy. As soon as the robot starts its trajectory in real indoor environments with obstacles, the sensor continuously detects and updates the occupancy map by the logsig strategy. A Gaussian function is used for modelling the ultrasonic sensor with the aim of reaching higher precision of the distance measured for each obstacle in the scene. Experiments on detecting, mapping and avoiding obstacles are performed using the mobile robotic platform DaNI 2.0 and the VxWorks system. The resulted occupancy grid is analysed and discussed at the end of this document.

Keywords: occupancy map, obstacle detection, path planning, robot mobile navigation, Gaussian model

1. Introduction

Nowadays, the artificial intelligent field has developed service task in robotic systems with the aim of providing help or comfort to humans. This is called service robotic [1], and it is supposed that the robot acts total or partially with autonomy. In particular, the service robotic tackles the problem of domestic robots. Such robots require highly autonomy and real-time processing for recognizing unknown environments. To do this, they use stereovision [2] and laser range finders [3, 4]. Furthermore, these robots must be able to autolocalizing and to navigate without human supervision, detect and locate obstacles and constructing its own map of the environment, using only their sensors and eventually a communication system with a central computer. The environment and workspace of the industrial robots are especially adapted for them and for performing special tasks; thus, these robots are programmed for knowing the environment in accordance with their physical dimensions. On the contrary, service robotics interacts with a changing and initially unknown environment.

Topologic and geometric maps could be constructed for perceiving robot environment. As proposed by Thrun et al. [5], a topologic map contains nodes and lines that joint these nodes representing the possible trajectories from one node to another. Furthermore, the author proposes the efficient mapping of the space and the low complexity as advantages, however, to recognize the place is difficult, depends of personal interpretation, and it could produce suboptimal trajectories. In contrast, the geometric maps numerically represent the coordinates and properties of the environment of the robot. These maps could efficiently represent big regions with few numeric parameters. Thus, the environment is descripted through geometric characteristics such as segments, corners, among others and their corresponding relationships (distance positions) [6].

On the other hand, the occupancy grid is a technique based on the discretization of the space in equal cells with a probability, which represents an occupied, empty or unknown area. This technique has been largely used due to it requires basic concepts for constructing, representing and updating and it allows to compute shorter trajectories. The main disadvantage of the occupancy grid is that requires the robot position.

The ultrasound is mechanical radiations with frequency higher to the audible range (>20 kHz) when these waves are reflected by an object in the environment. The ultrasonic sensors contain a piezoelectric transducer that is used as a transmitter and receptor for emitting and receiving the ultrasonic waves, respectively. This project proposes a strategy focused on ultrasonic sensors since this provides the distance from each obstacle in the environment to the sensor mounted on the robot. Recently, a self-configuring network of ultrasonic sensors has been proposed for tracking moving target [7], providing that these sensors provide an economical and basic solution to object detection in indoor environments.

In the development of novel strategies for proposing autonomous robotic systems, this work tackles with the problem of obstacle detection and avoiding in real time using an ultrasonic sensor embedded in a robot mobile during indoor navigation [8]. The environment is initially unknown; thus, first of all, the robot constructs an initial version of a two-dimensional (2D) occupancy map. Several experimental tests are performed for modelling the sensor error and for measuring the precision of measurements with the aim of assuring a reliable map.

2. Overall strategy for robot navigation

Figure 1 depicts the block diagram of the global strategy for constructing a local occupancy map of indoor environments. As the operating range of the ultrasonic sensor is known, this sets the size of the area covered by the sensor, which will be directly updated in the local map at each instant time *t*. This area establishes the size of an initial local map previously provided to the robot. On the other hand, before robot starts to move, the ultrasonic sensor is used for detecting objects in front of him. To do this, the ultrasonic sensor carries out a "sweep" in the range −90° to 90° with respect to X axis of the robot (see **Figure 2a**). The local map also uses the initial robot location, due to location of the objects are given with respect to the ultrasonic sensor. The path-planning module computes an initial path for robot navigation. The potential field's technique is used to plan the best trajectory for the robot. In real time, robot odometric location is obtained from the encoders for updating the map and continuously constructing the global map of the robot scene. Both global and local maps store the probability of occupancy around the robot during navigation.

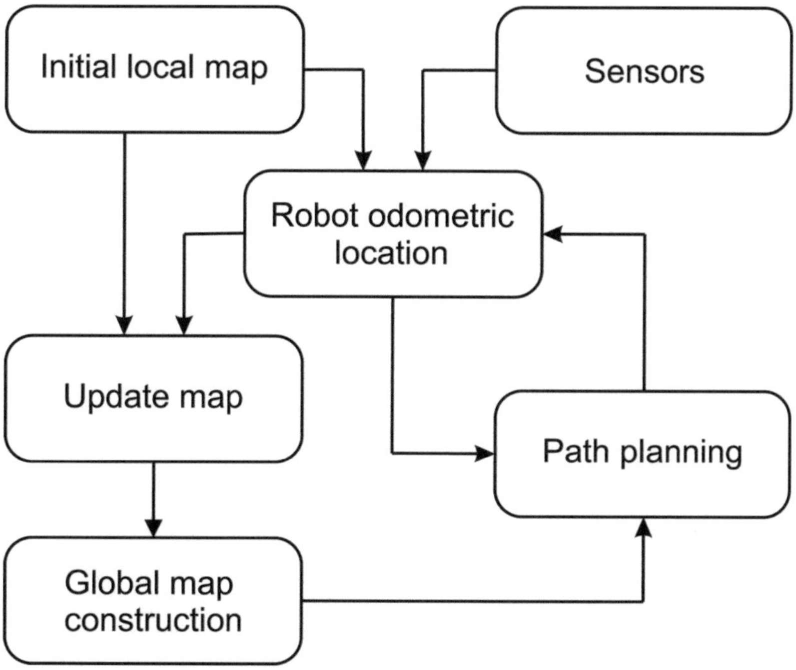

Figure 1. Global strategy for constructing an occupancy map during indoor navigation.

Every update of the global map is stored in a file internally on the robot. The map construction consists in dividing the environment in small uniform cells, which will be labelled as occupied or free in accordance with the ultrasonic measures. An intensive calibration strategy is required with the aim of obtaining an accurate digital representation of the real scene. The robot navigates from a predefined initial position to a goal position; then, the algorithm ends when the robot reaches such predefined goal position.

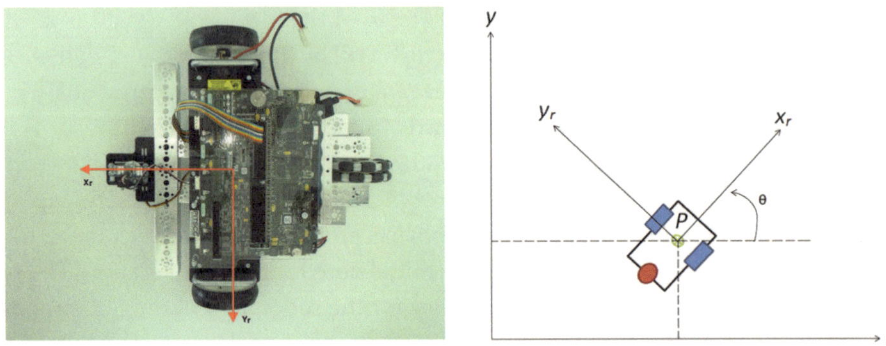

(a) (b)

Figure 2. (a) Reference axis of the mobile robot DaNI 2.0. (b) Graphical representation of the robot in the local and global reference axis, P represents the reference point of the position.

3. Robot model description

The mobile robot used in this project is shown in **Figure 2a**. This is a robotic platform called NI LabVIEW robotics Starter Kit® [9], also known as DaNI 2.0, developed by National Instruments company® (NI). This mobile robot was designed to develop and run algorithms in real time for autonomous system applications. The components of the mobile robot DaNI 2.0 are essentially: two DC motors, two encoders and a reconfigurable card sbRIO-9632 (Single Board Reconfigurable I/O), an ultrasonic sensor mounted on a servomotor for providing to sensor rotational motion. **Figure 2b** illustrates a graphical representation of the robot, with the global and local reference axis of the robot. The X and Y axes are defined arbitrarily in the plane as the reference of the global coordinates.

The kinematic model of the robot DaNI 2.0 consists in a differential configuration: each wheel of the robot is connected to a DC motor, which provides the traction force and a stabilization wheel for balancing the robot. The basic model for representing the robot position considers the robot as a single point in the space. Thus, the robot position is specified by choosing a point *P* in the robot chassis as a reference; usually, this point is the centre of the wheel axis. In addition, the point *P* represents the origin of the robot axis X_r and Y_r indicating the local reference of the robot position, see **Figure 2a**.

In particular, the sbRIO-9632 card is a heterogeneous-embedded platform, developed by NI®, which contains a real-time processor and serves as main control unit of the robot. Besides, this platform includes a Field Programming Gate Array (FPGA) Xilinx Spartan-3, which is a reconfigurable device that executes programmed tasks in real time, that is, the active response

http://dx.doi.org/10.5772/64871

of the system to external events. This real-time execution uses a low-level programming to perform tasks, such as motor control, signal acquisition by means of digital or analogue inputs and monitoring digital and analogue inputs/outputs, among others. However, a higher level of programming is possible through the NI LabVIEW® robotics software, which is a graphical language. Programming languages such as C, C++ or Java could be also used.

3.1. Robot odometric localization

During navigation, the robot needs to know its position and orientation with respect to its local and global axis of reference. To do this, the most common method used is based on geometric equations providing an estimation of the robot location by combining information obtained from the encoders on the wheels and from the propulsion components. This method is known as odometric estimation [10], and it is commonly used due to it only employs the kinematic model of the robot without including forces or torques in the mechanism. The main constraint of this method is that, a small error at the beginning of the estimation increases with the time, due to it is accumulated. Another strategy for avoiding this incremental error is to correct the robot position at regular times of movement, using landmarks [11]. Nevertheless, the cost of installation of the landmarks could be considerably high. For this reason, the odometric location strategy is commonly used providing enough results in short trajectories at low cost.

In order to compute the robot position $P(X, Y)$ in the global coordinate system, it is necessary to know the rotational angle between the local and global coordinate axis, given by θ and the origin coordinates of the robot local axis. The geometric equations for computing the point P position in global coordinates are as follows:

$$\begin{cases} X = X_r \cos(\theta) \\ Y = Y_r \sin(\theta) \end{cases} \tag{1}$$

The robot motion d_r is computed over the time by considering the robot geometry and its angular velocity on the wheels, using the following equation:

$$d_r = \frac{2\pi r}{rev} \varphi_{\omega} t \tag{2}$$

where r is the wheel radius (1.16 dm for the DaNI 2.0 robot), φ_{ω} the angular velocity of the wheel and t is the time.

In accordance with the robot geometry and the wheel type, the movement of the robot X_r is only in one direction (X direction is used). Furthermore, in the case of one wheel is keeping fix to the floor, while the second wheel moves with an angular velocity; then, the robot will draw a circle around the fixed wheel with a radius of $2l$; being l the distance from the point P in the chassis to the wheel (1.778 dm for DaNI 2.0 robot). This movement only affects θ angle:

$$\theta = \frac{r\varphi_{\omega}t}{2l} \tag{3}$$

In order to estimate the location errors due to the odometry, a square trajectory was implemented on the robot. It was found that such errors in the trajectory are mainly due to the errors in the turns, performed to 86° approximately but expected to 90°. Besides, small changes in the wheels' trajectory are not registered by the encoders, these changes are minimal, and however, they produce a notable final error.

The odometric errors exist essentially due to the robot construction, that is, there is a small difference between the diameters of the wheels. Furthermore, the finite resolution of the encoders and the irregularities in the floor where the trajectory is performed avoid an ideal execution of the trajectory.

3.2. Ultrasonic sensors

As it was mentioned in the introduction section, the ultrasonic sensors consist of one transmitter and receptor of the sound. Once the ultrasonic wave has been sent, when such wave found an object a signal, this is reflected as an echo and can be detected by the same transmitter, which acting also like a receptor. In general, the applications of the ultrasonic sensors are based on estimate the lapse of time between such emission and reception of the ultrasonic waves. This lapse of time is known as time of flight (ToF), the corresponding distance to the object that reflected the wave is estimated by means of:

$$d = \frac{1}{2} v \cdot t_f \tag{4}$$

where v represents the velocity of sound and t_f the time of flight.

On the other hand, one particular problem with the ultrasonic sensors is the mirror reflection. This reflection happens mainly in the corners and it is occasioned for several reflections of the ultrasonic waves before to return to the sensor (see **Figure 3**). As a consequence of this phenomenon, some objects of the environment of small size or orientation cannot be detected by the sensor, or in some cases, they are detected farther than really they are. Thus, only the readings taken when the ultrasonic wave impacts perpendicular to the surface will be taken as correct measures.

The cone of sensibility, also known as acoustic sensor aperture, introduces incertitude in the position and distance of the reflected object if the robot is in motion. This is illustrated in **Figure 4**: if one object is detected in the cone of sensibility, therefore, the measured distance will correspond to an object "in front" of the sensor, even if the object is located with an orientation with respect to the robot.

http://dx.doi.org/10.5772/64871

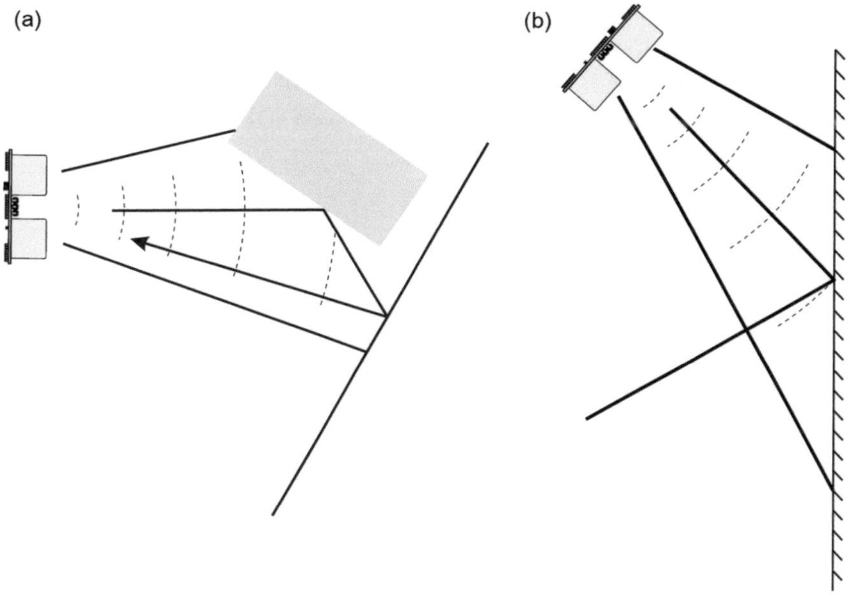

Figure 3. Mirror reflection of the ultrasonic waves. (a) Extended trajectory of the ultrasonic wave. (b) Ultrasonic echo that does not return to sensor.

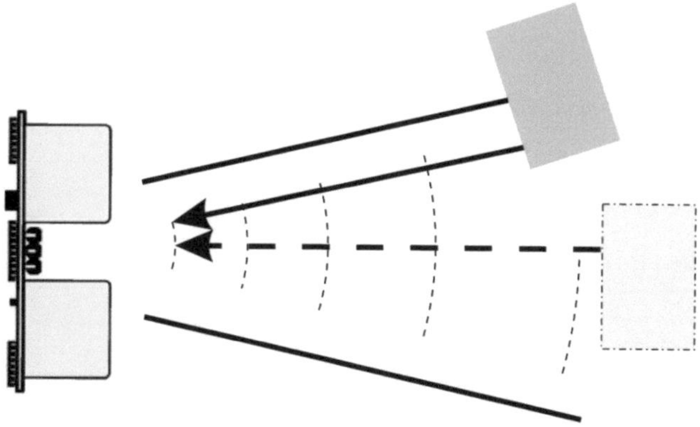

Figure 4. Main effect of the acoustic aperture of the ultrasonic sensor that produces incertitude in the object position, positioning the object in an unreal location.

3.3. Gaussian model of the ultrasonic sensor

The experimental test for modelling the sensor was performed at different sampling times with the aim of considering the effect of the robot motion in the measurements. The sampling times used were 60, 80, 100, 200 and 400 ms, in the range of −65° to 65° with intervals of 5° at distances of 6, 8 and 10 dm from the wall. **Figure 5** illustrates the average of these different test performed using a sampling time of 80 ms. The chart (a) shows a stable range of measurements among

−20° to 40° confirmed by the standard deviation shown in chart (b). Note that different sensor positions (6, 8 and 10 dm) do not affect the measurements. Similar results have been obtained for a sampling time of 100 ms; however, as this project will be performed in real time, 80 ms was chosen due to it represents the best trade-off between stability and time of detection.

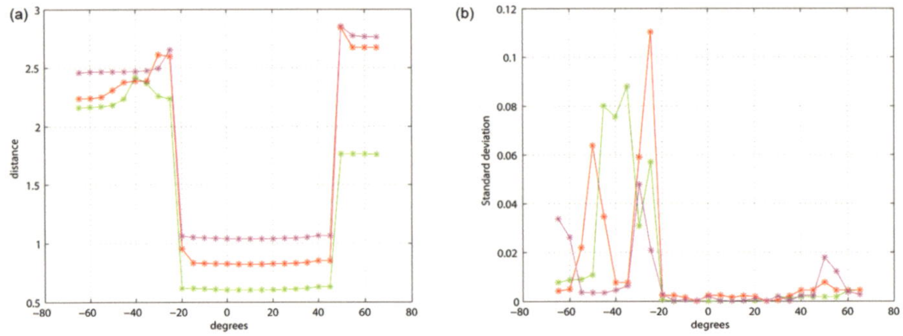

Figure 5. Charts of the measurement averages. (a) The sampling time used is 80 ms, for three distances 6, 8 and 10 dm. (b) The standard deviation of measurements performed in chart (a), note the range of stability is among −20° to 40°.

In order to reduce the measurement error of the ultrasonic sensor and to validate that the detected object is inside a specific region, it is used a probabilistic technique based on a Gaussian function. The Gaussian model implies to know the errors due to the distance and angle detection [12]. This model considers the measured distance, denoted here as d, and its uncertainty (σ_d), and orientation angle θ and its uncertainty (σ_θ). Therefore, the real measure is in the range of $d \pm \sigma_d$, and the orientation $\theta \pm \sigma_\theta$ is denoted by:

$$P(z|d,\theta) = \frac{1}{2\pi\sigma_d\sigma_\theta} e^{\left(\frac{-(d-z)^2}{2\sigma_d^2} + \frac{\theta^2}{\sigma_\theta^2}\right)} \tag{5}$$

where z is the variable in the workspace of the ultrasonic sensor measurements. This equation represents the probability that the object be in the position measured by the sensor and uses two standard deviations, range and angle (see **Figure 6a**). The error measured on the angle for one object located at 10 dm is 0.12 dm that represents an error of ±0.7°. This effect is small; therefore, it will be ignored for constructing the occupancy map, considering only the 1D model based on distance only (see Eq. 5). **Figure 6b** depicts in blue the 1D model of the ultrasonic sensor considering only the distance and the uncertainty (σ_d). Using a confiability value of 0.8, the resulted plot is shown in green. Once the object has been detected, the environment behind him is unknown. Thus, the probability of such cells is considered 0.5 because the cell value cannot be known (red plot in **Figure 6b**). Furthermore, this plot represents the probability of the object be in the distance describe in the x axis. This result will be used for occupancy map construction.

http://dx.doi.org/10.5772/64871

$$P(d|z) = \frac{1}{\sqrt{2\pi\sigma}} e^{\left(\frac{-(d-z)^2}{2\sigma^2}\right)} \tag{6}$$

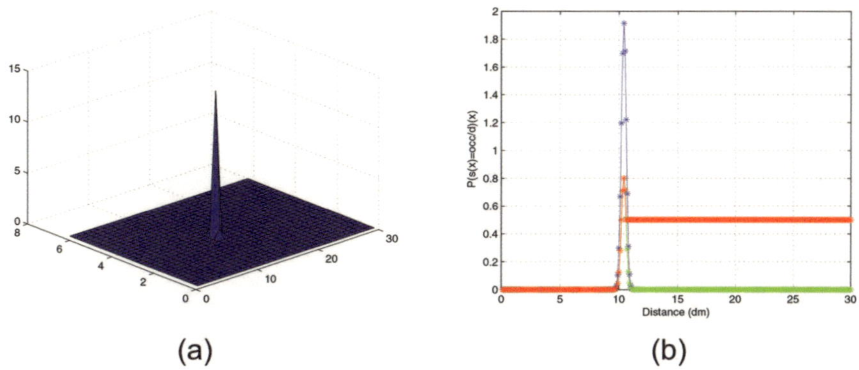

Figure 6. Gaussian model of the ultrasonic sensor. (a) Object position in coordinates (d, θ) for a 2D probability model. (b) Probability model of object position detected by ultrasonic sensor in 1D.

4. Global map construction

The occupancy maps are a probabilistic technique based on small cells that divide the surrounding space of the indoor or outdoor environments. The probability of one cell is occupied which is estimated using robot sensors. Each cell in the map represents the information contained in the physical space in front of the sensors used to measure the environment. The values in the cell describe the following situations:

$$\begin{cases} <0.5 & \text{free cell} \\ =0.5 & \text{unknown} \\ >0.5 & \text{occupied cell} \end{cases} \tag{7}$$

4.1. Static occupancy map

The initial local map uses the initial position of the robot, which is always knowing as navigation is performed only in indoor environments for constructing a static occupancy map considering that the robot is not moving in the environment. The ultrasonic sensor in front of the robot rotates in the range of −90° to 90° with respect to the x axis of the robot; nevertheless, the real range used was in the range of −20° to 40° in order to acquire more stable and accurate measures. Another advantage is that a reduced amount of measurements avoiding synchronization problems and allowing the real-time execution. The rest of the angle range will be covered as the robot navigates in the environment.

In this work, an initial local map is constructed since a static position of the robot in the environment which is represented by a grid as illustrated in **Figure 7b**. This map indicates the starting point of the robot trajectory and the corresponding state of the surrounding environment in accordance with Eq. (7). Each cell of the map represents 1 dm^2 of the environment minimizing the location errors due to the odometry of the robot. Note that, the red cells in the front and in both sides of the robot represent the obstacles in the scene (probability of the cells are higher to 0.5). This map is updated based on the log-odds algorithm for mapping the environment in a global map.

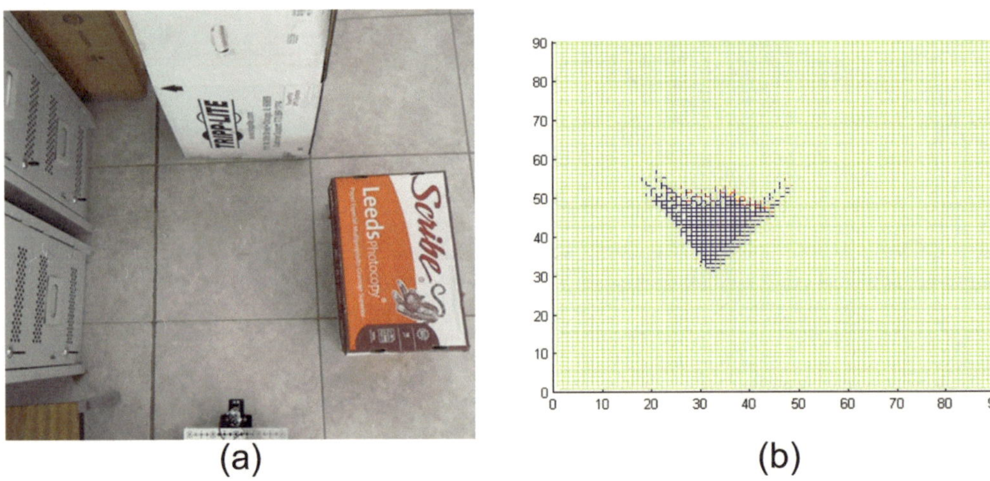

Figure 7. Initial local map. (a) Indoor scene with obstacle, (b) blue cells represent free space, red cells represent obstacles and green cells are unknown space.

4.2. Dynamic occupancy map

Figure 8 illustrates the block diagram for constructing the dynamic occupancy map. The measures obtained from the encoders in order to locate the robot in the global reference system. Once the current robot location in the environment is known, a homogenous transformation is carried out with the aim of updating the cells covered by the ultrasonic sensor based on the Eq. (7) and finally assigning them in the global map.

Note that, in the odometric localization block of **Figure 8**, the local reference axis of the robot has been rotated and angle β with respect to global axis. Therefore, one point (X_1, Y_1) in the local robot axis oriented with an angle α will be located in the global reference axis by means of:

$$\begin{bmatrix} X \\ Y \\ 1 \end{bmatrix} = \begin{bmatrix} \cos\alpha & -\sin\alpha & O_X \\ \sin\alpha & \cos\alpha & O_Y \\ 0 & 0 & 1 \end{bmatrix} \begin{bmatrix} X_1 \\ Y_1 \\ 1 \end{bmatrix} \tag{8}$$

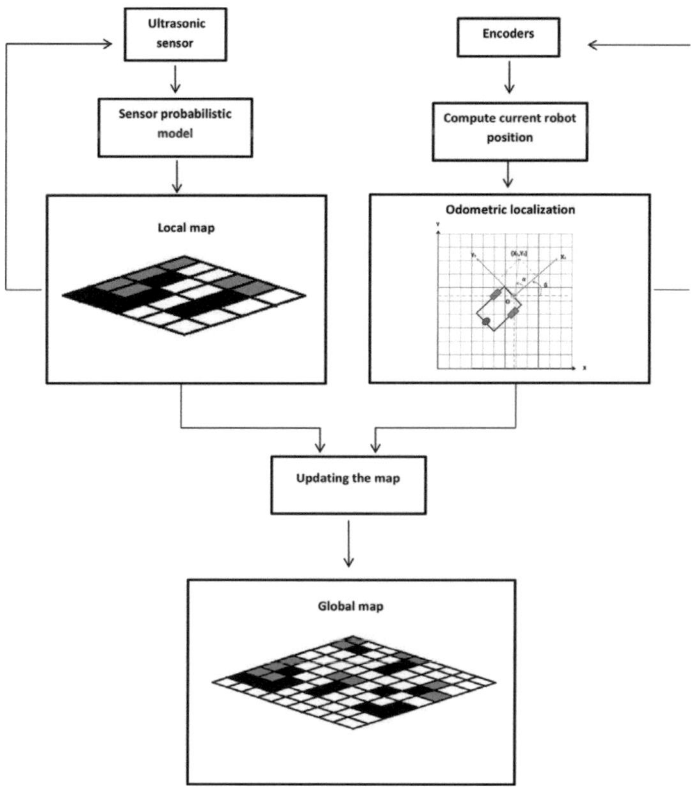

Figure 8. Local and global reference axis for constructing the dynamic occupancy map.

4.3. Updating the global map

One commonly used technique for updating the occupancy map is the Bayesian strategy, described in Eq. (10), which defines the probability P of the cell state $s(C_i)$ be occupied, given the distance (d) measured by the sensor at the time $t+1$.

$$P\left[s(C_i) = OCC|_{d_{t+1}}\right] = \frac{P\left[d_{t+1}|s(C_i) = OCC\right]P\left[s(C_i) = OCC|d_t\right]}{\sum_{s(C_i)} P\left[d_{t+1}|s(C_i)\right]P[s(C_i)|d_t]} \tag{9}$$

Each lecture provides partial information of the environment; therefore, in order to establish the state of each cell, an updated equation is used for combining the prior and the current probabilities of the cell, yielding:

$$P(C_i) = P(C_i)_{t-1} + P(C_i)_t \tag{10}$$

4.4. The log-odds algorithm

Eq. (10) could give numerical instabilities for probabilities closer to 0 or 1. To overcome this problem, Thrun [13] propose that the status "occupied" for each cell i at instant time t can be modelled as the logarithm of an occupied cell, divided by the probability of the cell be empty and represented by:

$$l_{t,i} = \log \frac{P\left[\left(C_i\right) | d\right]}{1 - P\left[\left(C_i\right) | d\right]} \tag{11}$$

The probability could be obtained, easily:

$$P\left(C_i\right) = 1 - \frac{1}{1 - e^{l_{t,i}}} \tag{12}$$

Besides, it is considered that the prior value of the occupied cells l_0 takes a constant value given by:

$$l_0 = \log \frac{P(C_i = 1)}{P(C_i = 0)} = \log \frac{P(C_i)}{1 - P(C_i)} \tag{13}$$

The algorithm for updating the occupancy map is described as follows:

Algorithm 1. Updating the occupancy map

Inputs: $\{l_{t-1,i}, r, z\}$

for each cell C_i do

if C_i is in the vision field of the sensor then

$l_{t,i} = l_{t-1,i} + l_{sensor\_model} - l_0$

else

$l_{t,i} = l_{t-1,i}$

end if

end for

5. Path planning

A safe and coherent navigation of the robot in his workspace requires a path planning technique and an obstacle avoidance strategy. In this project, the path planning technique used

http://dx.doi.org/10.5772/64871

is the potential fields which basically consist in the computation of the attraction forces produced by the goal position and the repulsion forces caused by the closer objects in the scenario. Thus, an artificial potential field guides the robot to goal position, while the obstacle avoidance method allows a safe navigation of the robot.

The potential field acting on the robot is given by the attraction field towards the goal and the repulsion field produced by the obstacles, that is:

$$U(q) = U_{\text{att}}(q) + U_{\text{rep}}(q) \quad (14)$$

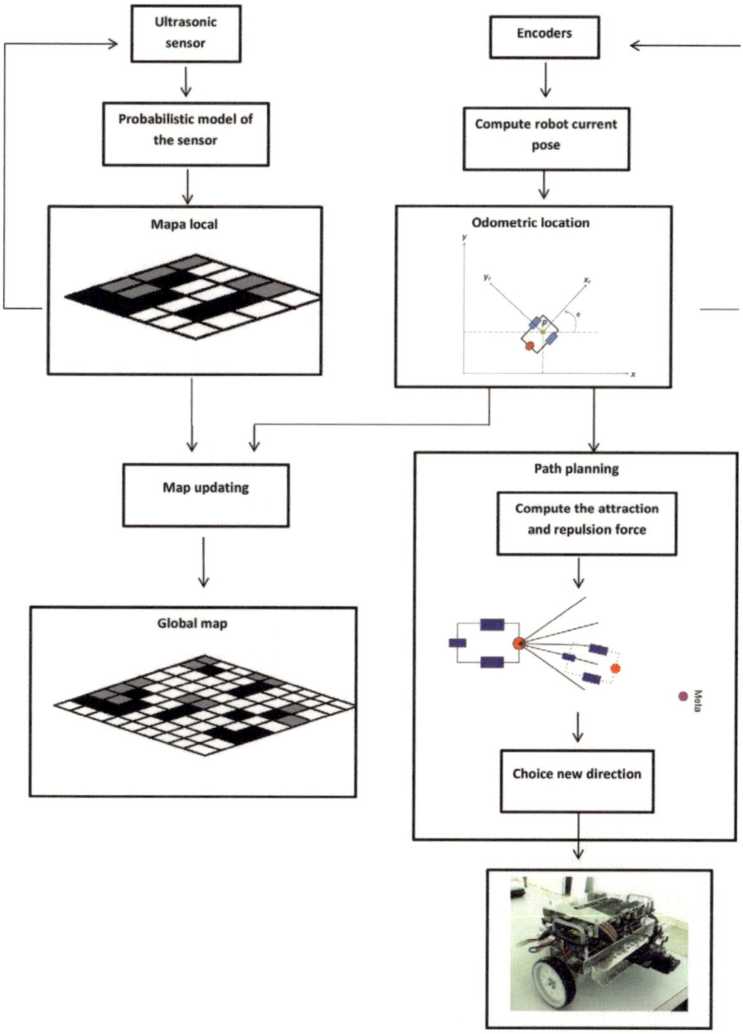

Figure 9. Block diagram of the path planning algorithm.

In the same way, the forces could be separated in attraction and repulsion forces yielding:

$$F(q) = F_{\text{att}}(q) - U_{\text{rep}}(q) \tag{15}$$

Furthermore, the attraction force could be described as:

$$F_{\text{att}}(q) = -k_{\text{att}} \cdot \left|\left(q - q_{\text{goal}}\right)\right| \tag{16}$$

where $\rho_{goal}(q)$ is the Euclidean distance between $\| q - q_{goal} \|$, and the repulsion force could be described as:

$$F_{\text{rep}}(q) = \begin{cases} \frac{1}{2} k_{\text{rep}} \left(\frac{1}{\rho(q)} - \frac{1}{\rho_0} \right) \frac{1}{\rho^2(q)} \frac{q - q_{\text{obstacle}}}{\rho(q)} & si\, \rho(q) \leq \rho_0 \\ 0 & si\, \rho(q) \geq \rho_0 \end{cases} \tag{17}$$

where k_{att} and k_{rep} are positive scalar factors, $\rho(q)$ is the minimal distance from q to the object and ρ_0 is the distance in which an object influences in the path.

The general strategy for programming the path planning algorithm is illustrated in **Figure 9**. If the current robot position is known, then the resultant force is estimated considering all the new directions that the robot can take. Such directions are chosen based on the angle of observation of the ultrasonic sensor and the probable position of the robot if he walks in that specific direction. Once each force has been computed, the smaller is selected due to this force moves the robot closer to the goal. Once the new direction has been selected, the motors are turned on to follow this direction. The algorithm ends when the goal has been reached by the robot.

6. Experimental results

Several tests were performed to validate the path planning algorithm. In the tests, the mobile robot DaNI 2.0 navigates in an indoor environment with obstacles located between the starting and goal position. Both starting and goal positions are the same during the experiments and only the obstacle locations change. The graphical representation of the occupancy map is labelled as: green colour represents the unknown environment, blue cells represent free path (empty cells) and red cells represent obstacles (occupied cells).

The first experimental test is performed in an environment without obstacles; the results are illustrated in **Figure 10**. The odd rows of this figure show different instant times of the whole sequence performed by the robot; in particular, the first picture shows the starting position, and the ninth picture shows the goal position of the robot. Even rows depict the occupancy map constructed at that time. Note how effectively the obstacles detected are located in the borders of the region navigated by the robot, that is, any obstacle is detected in the middle of the scene as is expected.

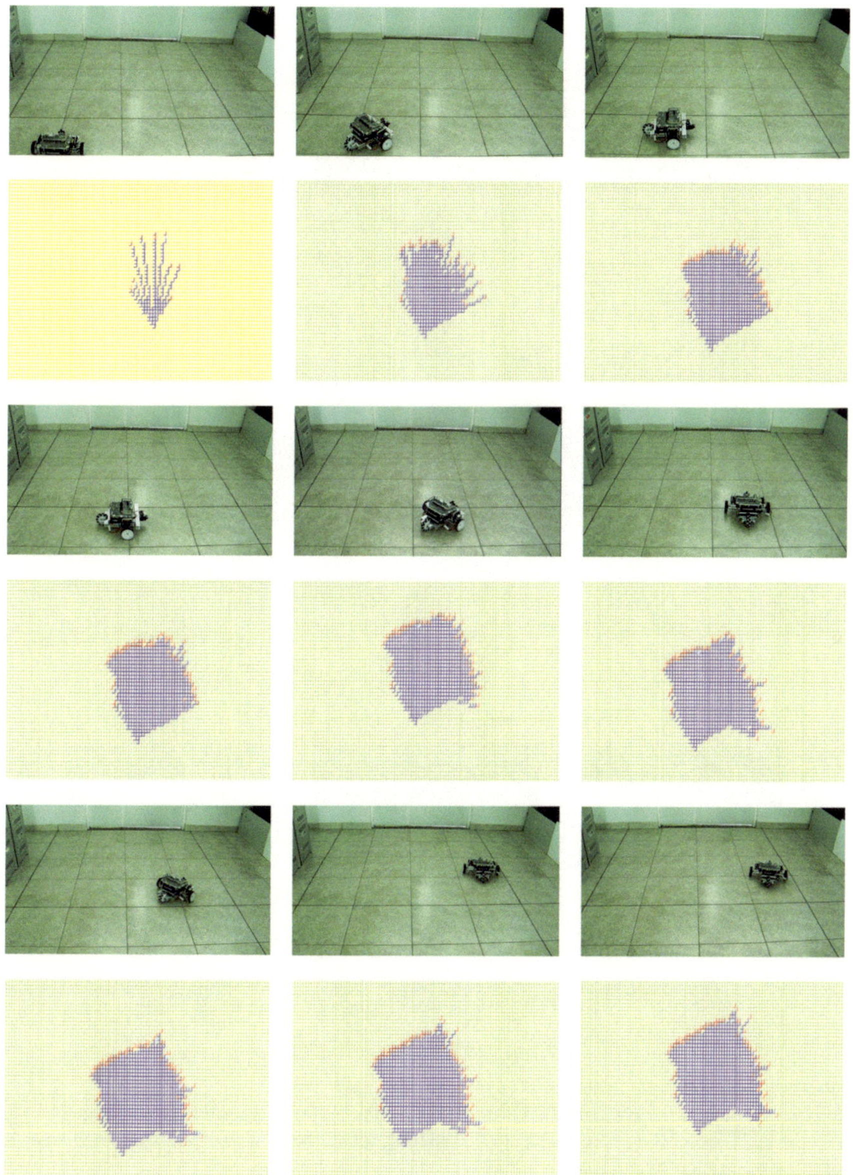

Figure 10. Test 1 of the path planning algorithm. The navigation is performed without obstacles. The graphical representation of the occupancy map is updating using the measurement obtained from the ultrasonic sensor, during robot navigation in real time.

The second experimental test is performed in an environment with two obstacles; the results are illustrated in **Figure 11**. In this case, the first picture shows the starting position, and the ninth picture shows the goal position of the robot. Note that the final occupancy map constructed is smaller than the map of the test 1. The last is due to obstacles are detected therefore included as red cells; however, behind the object, even if there are a free space, this area is not reached for the ultrasonic sensor.

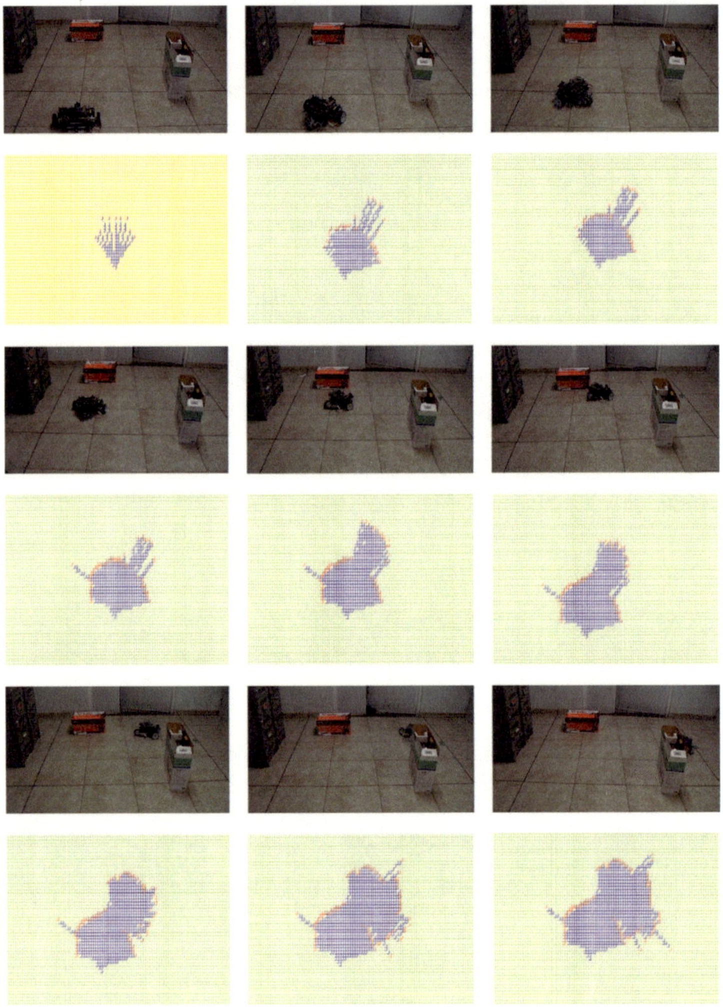

Figure 11. Test 2 of the path planning algorithm. The navigation is performed with two obstacles in the environment. The graphical representation of the occupancy map is updating using the measurements obtained from the ultrasonic sensor, during robot navigation in real time.

The results of the last experimental test showed here are illustrated in **Figure 12**. As in the test 2, the occupancy map is small with respect to the real environment due to zones behind objects cannot be not established by the robot.

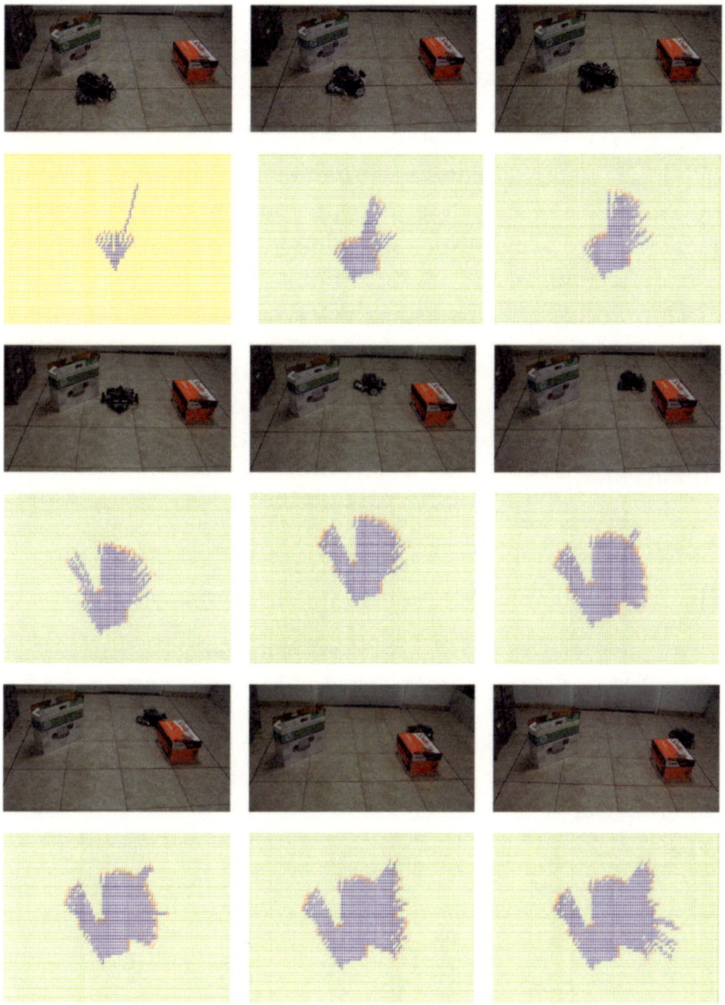

Figure 12. Test 3 of the path planning algorithm. The navigation is performed with two obstacles in the environment at different position with respect to test 2. The graphical representation of the occupancy map is updating using the measurements obtained from the ultrasonic sensor, during robot navigation in real time.

7. Conclusions and perspectives

The construction of occupancy map using ultrasonic sensors is easily perturbed by environmental noise. To overcome this constraint, it is used a Gaussian model of the sensor, providing higher precision of the distance measured for each obstacle in the scene. In addition, another typical error found in the measurements performed by ultrasonic sensors is related with the cone produced at the time of sending the ultrasonic signal. In this project, it was found that this error is less than 1°; therefore, it could be ignored. Furthermore, the error produced by the irregularities in the floor is reduced by using the proportional integral-derivative (PID) control of the robot. Updating the global map requires the synchronization between the ultrasonic measures and the robot location in the environment.

The occupancy map of a real indoor environment is constructed by an ultrasonic sensor and a mobile robot. The logsig strategy allows a safe indoor navigation of our robot by establishing a probability of occupancy to each cell in the map avoiding a collision of the robot with an obstacle. The global strategy is performed in real time. The time employed for the robot for constructing the map depends of the number of obstacle in the scene; however, a real-time execution of the platform is assured by using the VxWorks platform of the robot DaNI 2.0.

Future works are focused on multiple robot navigation on dynamic environments. To do this, a proposed approach consists in sending the local map constructed for one robot to a master terminal by IP connection in order to incrementally construct the global map by adding local maps of the environment.

Author details

Dora-Luz Almanza-Ojeda*, Yazmín Gomar-Vera and Mario-Alberto Ibarra-Manzano

*Address all correspondence to: luzdora@ieee.org

Electronics Engineering Department, DICIS, University of Guanajuato, Salamanca, Guanajuato, México

References

[1] Somolinos Sánchez J. A., editor. Advanced robotics and computer vision, 1st ed., Spain : Ediciones de la Universidad de la Mancha ; 2002. pp. 285 p.

[2] Tavera-Vaca C.-A., Almanza-Ojeda D.-L., Ibarra-Manzano M.-A. Analysis of the efficiency of the census transform algorithm implemented on FPGA. Microprocessors and Microsystem. 2015;39(7):494–503. doi:10.1016/j.micro.2015.08.002

[3] Ventura R., Ahmad A. Towards Optimal Robot Navigation in Domestic Spaces. In: Reinaldo A. C., Bianchi, H. Levent Akin, Subramanian Ramamoorthy, Komei Sugiura, editors. RoboCup 2014: Robot World Cup XVIII. 1st ed. Switzerland: Springer; 2015. p. 318–331. doi:10.1007/978-3-319-18615-3_26

[4] Martínez M. A., Martínez J. L., Morales J. Motion Detection from Mobile Robots with Fuzzy Threshold Selection in Consecutive 2D Laser Scans. Electronics, 2015 ; 4(1) : 82-93. Doi : 10.3390/electronics40110082

[5] Thrun S., Burgard W., Fox D. Probabilistic Robotics. 1st ed. Cambridge, MA: The MIT Press; 2005. pp. 672 p.

[6] Leonard J. J., Durrant-Whyte H. F. Mobile robot localization by tracking geometric beacons. IEEE Transactions on Robotics and Automation. 1991;7(3):376–382. doi: 10.1109/70.88147

[7] Teixido M., Palleja T., Font D., Tresanchez M., Moreno J., Palacin J. Two-Dimensional radial laser scanning for circular marker detection and external mobile robot tracking. Sensors. 2012;12(12):16482–16497. doi:10.3390/s121216482

[8] Almanza Ojeda D. L., Gomar Vera Y., Ibarra Manzano M. A. Obstacle Detection and avoidance by a mobile robot using probabilistic models. IEEE Latin America Transactions. 2015;13(1):69–75. doi:10.1109/TLA.2015.7040630

[9] National Instruments. LabVIEW Robotics [Internet]. 05/01/2016 [Updated: 05/01/2016]. Available from: http://sine.ni.com/psp/app/doc/p/id/psp-912/lang/es [Accessed: 05/15/2016]

[10] Klarer P. 2D Navigation for Wheeled Vehicles. 1st ed. Albuquerque: Sandia National Laboratories; 1998.

[11] Borenstein J., Feng L., Everett. Where am I? Sensors and Methods for Autonomous Mobile Robot Localization. 1st ed. Michigan: The University of Michigan; 1994.

[12] Kuc R., Barshan B. Navigating vehicles through an unstructured environment with sonar. In: IEEE, editor. IEEE International Conference Robotics and Automation; 24–29 May 1989; Scottsdale, AZ. IEEE; 1989. p. 1422–1426. doi:10.1109/ROBOT.1989.100178

[13] Thrun S. Learning metric-topological maps for indoor mobile robot navigation. Artificial Intelligence. 1998;99(1):21–71. doi:10.1016/S0004-3702(97)00078-7

Chapter 5

Analysis of a Sorter Cascade Applied to Control a Wheelchair

Marcos Figueredo , Alexandre Nascimento ,
Roberto L.S. Monteiro and Marcelo A. Moret

Additional information is available at the end of the chapter

http://dx.doi.org/10.5772/63816

Abstract

The precise eye state detection is a fundamental stage for various activities that require human-machine interaction (HMI). This chapter presents an analysis of the implementation of a system for navigating a wheelchair with automation (CRA), based on facial expressions, especially eyes closed using a Haar cascade classifier (HCC). Aimed at people with locomotor disability of the upper and lower limbs, the state detection was based on two steps: the capture of the image, which concentrates on the detection actions and image optimization; actions of the chair, which interprets the data capture and sends the action to the chair. The results showed that the model has excellent accuracy in identification with robust performance in recognizing eyes closed, bypassing well occlusion issues and lighting with about 98% accuracy. The application of the model in the simulations opens the implementation and marriage opportunity with the chair sensor universe aiming a safe and efficient navigation to the user.

Keywords: wheelchair, classifier cascade, detector eyes closed, active vision, eyes state

1. Introduction

A number of illnesses and accidents can lead to severe damage in the spinal cord of a patient resulting in the loss of motion in the lower and upper parts. According to [1], 14% of the population has some kind of disability, be it visual, motor, hearing, and others, representing a growth of 7% in recent years.

Among this group, about 4% do not have any kind of movement in the lower and upper limbs. This is due to very serious motor problems, such as hemiplegia of four members and the need for ventilatory support. Also applies to patients with degenerative diseases of the neuromuscular system, for example, amyotrophic lateral sclerosis (ALS) in which in a progressive manner the person loses his movements, until completely paralyzed, thereby causing death by respiratory failure.

Among the various types of motor disabilities that can affect a person, quadriplegia (motor disability of the four members) and the neuromotor system diseases such as ALS are serious deficiencies, which lead the individual to an almost vegetative state, with difficulties with integration into society as useful as a capable person. However, in most cases such individuals have full brain capacity, and with the necessary physical media, they may participate productively in society. Thus, it is necessary to find ways to develop their personal and professional skills and have a professional activity with human dignity.

Typically, this patient uses a wheelchair to perform tasks such as come and go, always with the aid of a carer or relative. Some of these use couplings that allow the user to their locomotion in their environment and in general are very invasive.

The works of [2–5] indicate the concern of the academic community in realizing technology stocks, low cost, that make the everyday life of these more independent people, and these studies also indicate that these actions prolong the lives of patients and improve their quality of life [6, 7].

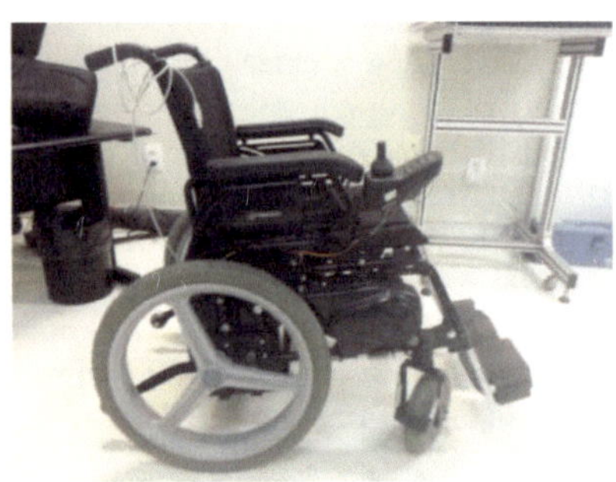

Figure 1. CRA used as prototype.

Several studies have been conducted by different research groups [8–10] to develop wheelchairs with some kind of intelligence or are simply able to understand voice commands, autonomous locomotion, deviation obstructions, and other functions as outlined in [2]. These models have a high cost and maintenance, having little or no type of embedded technology.

Motivated by this reality began an interdisciplinary nature project that aims to provide a common wheelchair with elements that make it both possible and economically viable the mobility of a patient without movements of the upper and lower limbs. Patients with this degree of disability have only a means of interaction with the machine elements present in one's face, which will are the facial expressions and the device that will allow the mobility automation with wheelchair (CRA), as shown in **Figure 1**.

This navigation is limited in some aspects, as some movements of facial expressions were extremely tiring, such as opening and closing the mouth, and others were too difficult to be captured or required equipment that are still under development, such as the retina of the eye movement. So two expressions have proved less susceptible to failure, namely low intrusiveness and low learning curve. They are the opening and closing of the eyes and the movement of turning one's head to right and left. These expressions were evaluated by 20 individuals simulating the state of a quadriplegic and generated evaluation described in **Table 1**.

Facial expression	Failure (%)	Setting (%)	Intrusiveness (0–10)	Learning (0–10)
Close and open your eyes	2	98	2	2
Head spin	3	97	2	3

Table 1. Percentage of success and failure detection of facial expressions. Average score of the difficulty of learning to use facial expressions, and how this application was not intrusive or in a total of 20 individuals.

Hence, the model for navigating a CD is based on two expressions:

- Open and close your eyes (move the seat forward or stop);
- Turning the head to the left or right (moves the seat through 90° about the axis thereof)

This work aims to present the architecture to detect the action of opening and closing the eyes based on HCC characteristics and evaluate the performance of the detector according to efficiency and effectiveness.

The effectiveness of the detector was tested in the prototype, evaluating their response to commands, since its effectiveness was evaluated from:

- Target image database construction considering regionalities and Brazilian cultural diversity;
- Manipulation of the various training variables;
- Handling and controlling the ideal minimum number of neighbors of the detector, reducing the number of false positives;
- Increased response or equal to 98% accuracy.

According to [11], the model [12] uses a classifier cascade and features of HCC. It works great on face detection and has already become standard for its high hit rate and low false positive rate.

The model [12] is adaptive and widely used by its degree of robustness and speed. In our implementation, the detection is based on HCC, with parameters evaluated, and a positive bank with about 10,000 images of frontal eyes closed, as shown in **Figure 2**.

This chapter is organized as follows: Section 2 presents the state of the art related to work developed here as well as our contribution. Section 3 describes the materials and the method used for the realization and implementation of the architecture. Section 4 presents the tests and results. Section 5 in turn brings the conclusions and future work.

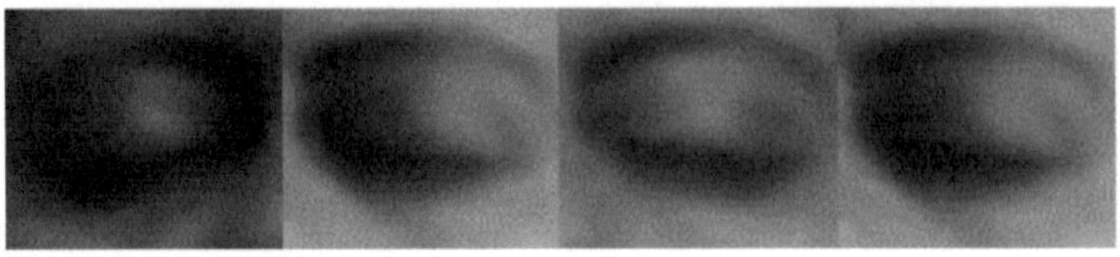

Figure 2. Sample det positive.

2. State of the art

According to [2], there are more than 35 CRI projects around the world, all of these projects vary in many ways. Initially, they include the project IntellWheels [2] which aims to create a development platform for intelligent wheelchairs, facilitating the design and testing of new methods and techniques for the CRIs, which takes as its premise aspects of low cost, comfort, and ergonomics.

Elizabeth and Roger [13] propose a seat which makes use of the head movement to perform navigation with a video system and a helmet with sensors. The study by [14] provides that the construction of an ellipsoidal 3D model of the head interprets the flow of this movement and establishes, according to the author, a more effective methodology than 2D approach.

Based on the Kalman filter to predict the possible movement of the head [15], attempts to reduce the action of the head movement assuming that with few moves the chair can now follow a route estimated by this position. This action, according to the author, reduces user effort.

Taylor and Nguyen [16] and Nguyen et al. [17] use similar ideas to use sensors placed on the user's head (especially accelerometers) to detect motion in a system designed to free platform. Wei-Kai and Isaac [18] address the recognition of facial gestures in interactive environments and aims to recognize the gestures through points of interest in the face of the individual by using Active Shape Models to extract face features to then assemble a 3D model in line with Actinos Facial Coding System (FACS).

Manogna et al. [19] create a system to directly control the engine speed based on the movement of the head. The device is fixed on the patient's head and sensor-based motion produces CRI. The same study was performed by [20], who evaluated a similar device in a closed environment. It describes the difficulty in understanding the face and his intentions and suggests using the same type of sensor.

The study by [19, 20] has been updated with the study by [21] that detects the opening and closing of the mouth for extra movement and studying the problem of head ergonomics. Zheng et al. [5] describe the Lucas-Kanade algorithm for detecting facial movement and discusses a method efficiency, accuracy, and response time.

http://dx.doi.org/10.5772/63816

Control of the CRA's status based on the opening and closing of the eyes is a simple method used to control the same as the state of the art analyzed but widely applied in research-related fatigue drivers to avoid traffic accidents.

Martin and colleagues [22, 23] describe a system that locates and tracks your eyes for algebraic operations on the face of the image extracted by the method of [20], which notably is also used in [24–30]. In all, eyes are found from the face detection which reduces the search space and facilitates significantly the detection task to then perform detection. Some utilize filters that improve the detection condition.

It is noticed that the utilization of computer vision for CRI movement was gradual. It was also almost constant that the use of accelerometers or cameras on the individual's head makes the equipment very intrusive and requires specific training to use the hardware and therefore difficult to adapt. The hit rates always fluctuate above 90%, but these mentioned, none is to analyze the influence of detector creation parameters. The majority does not have a specific database for the purpose and generally uses the same standard database available on the Web.

The contribution of this work is focused on the identification of the influence of the classifier training parameters and the relationship between complexity and efficiency/effectiveness of the detector.

Formation of a database of 10,000 images and analyze the influence of regionalism in the detector as opposed to embedded detectors in public libraries. The analysis of processing time both the detector's response to its creation.

3. Materials and method

The model for the detection of eye state uses a simple idea. If a detector can detect a human eye on a front face then it must also recognize one eye closed. To this end, a trained classifier cascade is used to identify this object in the input image. The choice of [12] model mainly provides for its simplicity, speed of execution, and the outstanding performance [8]. The method basically combines four key concepts:

- Rectangular features called Haar features;
- Full image;
- Learning algorithm—AdaBoost;
- A classifier cascade.

The combination of these ideas permits simultaneous selection of key features and trains the classifier cascade, and then next steps will be described.

3.1. Features of Haar

The Haar features encode the existence of contrasts between the targeted regions of the image. A set of these resources is used to encode the contrasts displayed by a human face, on this work, eyes closed, and their spatial relationships. These characteristics are called Haar, because its concept is similar to the coefficients of the Haar wavelet, set in a detection window W×H pixels according to the formula:

$$\text{features} = \sum_{i=1}^{N} \omega_i RecSum(r_i) \tag{1}$$

where ω_i is arbitrarily singling as weight factor, and **RecSum**(r_i) is the sum of the intensities of the pixels, which was described by [12] as a full image. The rectangle r_i and described as a function of five parameters:$\boldsymbol{r} = (x, y, w, h, \varphi)$, where x, y are the coordinates of the top position of the pixel array, w and h define the dimensions of the rectangle, and $\varphi = \{0°, 45°\}$ represents the degree of rotation.

The presence of a characteristic Haar, **Figure 3**, is determined by subtracting the average pixel value of the region by the average pixel value of the clear area. If the difference is above a threshold (set during learning), the characteristic is present.

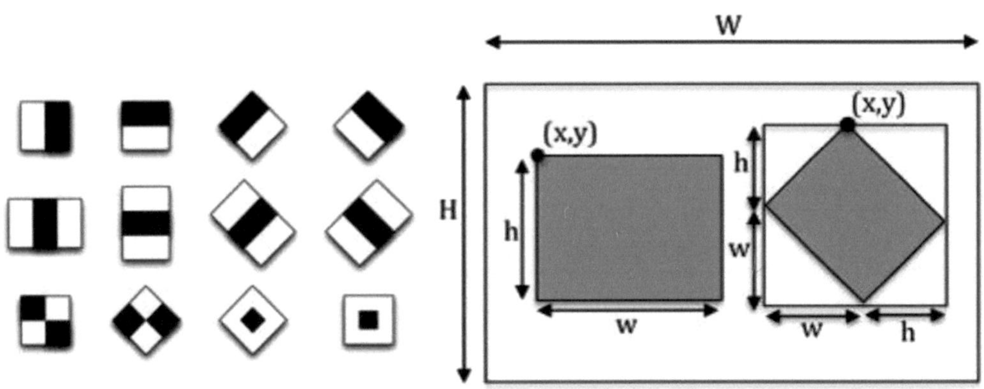

Figure 3. Some features of Haar and the detection window.

Paul and Michael [12] reported the fact that the choice of the characteristics of use, rather than models based on pixel points of the image statistics, is important because of the benefits of the ad hoc domain knowledge, which can be extracted knowledge hidden in images hardly found in a finite set of training.

In the case of blink detection, this fact is used to represent the approximate information and also related to the test image backgrounds. This knowledge becomes very thin with respect to open and closed eye, the use of the two is hardly found in other models with appearance-based approach.

In general, therefore, the characteristics are nothing more than rating information for a set of light intensity of a pixel. This process consists of the sum of the intensity of the pixels of white

http://dx.doi.org/10.5772/63816

regions of characteristics and the intensity subtracted from the sum of the gray balance of the image. The results are used as the characteristic value of a given location and can be combined to form weak hypotheses in the images [31].

Typically, the model adopts the rectangles seen in **Figure 3** and determines the presence or absence of thousands of Haar features in each image position and with different scales, Paul and Michael [12] used a technique called integral image.

3.2. Full image

The complete image created from the original image, a new representation of the image, simply sums the values of each pixel to the left and above, inclusively. The idea to use this representation is to increase the speed of feature extraction, as any rectangle of an image can be calculated by means of this idea. Only four indices are required to calculate any rectangle, and as an immediate consequence, one needs only one pass for desired data in subregions of an image, see **Figures 4** and **5**.

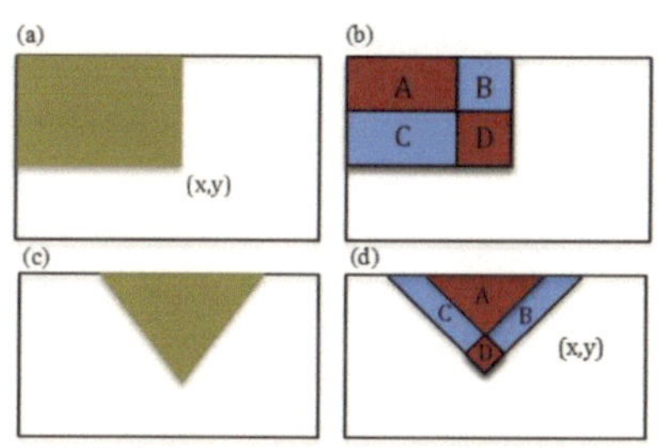

Figure 4. Representation of full image: (a) area calculation, (b) sum of areas A–B–C+D, (c) rationed area calculation, (d) quick sum A–B–C+D.

8	3	9	7	1
1	8	5	2	3
6	7	5	2	3
5	2	9	3	1
4	0	8	1	2

(a) Image input - A

0	0	0	0	0	0
0	8	11	20	27	28
0	9	20	34	43	47
0	15	33	52	63	73
0	20	40	68	82	93
0	24	44	80	95	108

(b) Integral image of A

Figure 5. Integral calculus image representation. It should be noted that the sum of the region (a) is equal to seven in (b) represented as 108–73–80+52.

3.3. Adaboost

The source Boosting problem in computational area, known as machine learning, can be exposed informally as follows: suppose there is a sorting method which is slightly better than a random choice for any distribution X, called weak learner or weak classifier. The existence of a classifier weak implies the existence of a strong classifier (strong learner), with small error on the entire space X.

In statistics, it is asked if given a reasonable estimation method, you can get a method close to great. This problem was solved by [32], which presented an algorithm that transforms a weak classifiers into a strong classifier.

From then on, several algorithms were developed within the context of boosting. One of the most recent and successful algorithms is known as AdaBoost that comes from the fact that boosting generates in every step a distribution on the observations of the sample and gives greater weight (most likely to be in the disturbed sample) to misclassified observations in the previous step. The basic algorithm is shown in **Figure 6**.

Algorithm 1: Basic model AdaBoost algorithm

Input: Take a sample: $\mathbb{S} = \{(x_i, y_i), x_i \in X, y_i \in \{-1, 1\}\}$

$w_1 \leftarrow u$

for $t = 1, 2, \ldots, T$ **do**

  Take $(h_t : X \to S) \leftarrow WL(\mathbb{S}, w_t)$;

  Find $\alpha_t \in \mathbb{R}$

  Update $\forall 1 \leqslant i \leqslant m$,

  $w_{t+1,i} \leftarrow w_{t,i}.e^{(-\alpha_t y_i h_t(x_i))/Z_t}$

Output: $H_T(x) = \sum_{t=1}^{T} \alpha_t h_t(x)$

Figure 6. Adaboost algorithm.

In this sense, AdaBoost is focused on the bad ratings, or else the data difficult to classify, and this is the main feature of this algorithm: minimize error over a training set. One of the advantages of AdaBoost, as studied by [33, 34], is the existence of other parameters, in addition to T shifts, to improve learning.

The result, after successive iterations of the algorithm, a set of hypotheses with weights wherein those having lower classification errors become more important, is called strong hypothesis or strong classifier.

3.4. Classifier cascaded

Increasing the speed of a classification task, in general, results in an increase in errors associated. However, for this purpose to be effective, we would have to reduce the number of evaluation of the weak classifiers, which would result in a loss in accuracy of the system. So Paul and Michael [12] propose a degenerative tree decision, decision stump, the structure that contains the binder thread from general to more specific, according to which the first cascade levels are not very accurate, although able to sort a large number of samples with a small amount of characteristics.

The use of cascade is characterized by the fact that, in an image during a detection task, the most sub-window analyzed by classifier is rejected. For this reason, a generalization in the early stages should be high enough to avoid the transition to subsequent stages of sub-windows classified as false positive [35], as shown in **Figure 7**.

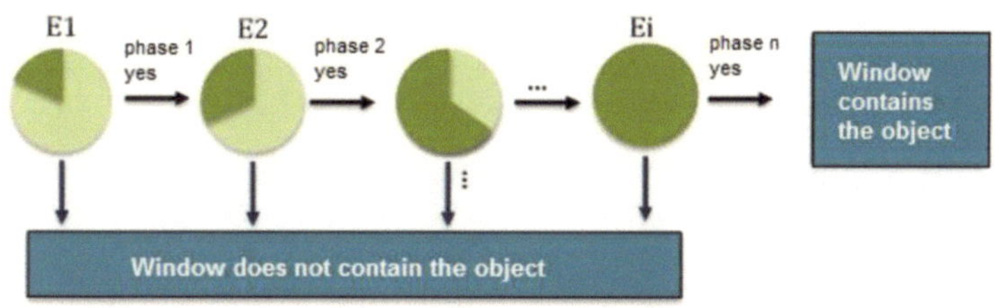

Figure 7. Estructure of the classifier.

3.5. The chair

One of the general proposed projects involves low cost as the minimum use of equipment is attached to the chair. This comprises only a webcam coupled to the PC and a Kinect® sensor (see **Figure 8**) coupled to the associated chair or independently allows the model to obtain various environmental information capable of determining actions of the chair, for example the sudden passage of someone in front of the same or the proximity of an obstacle.

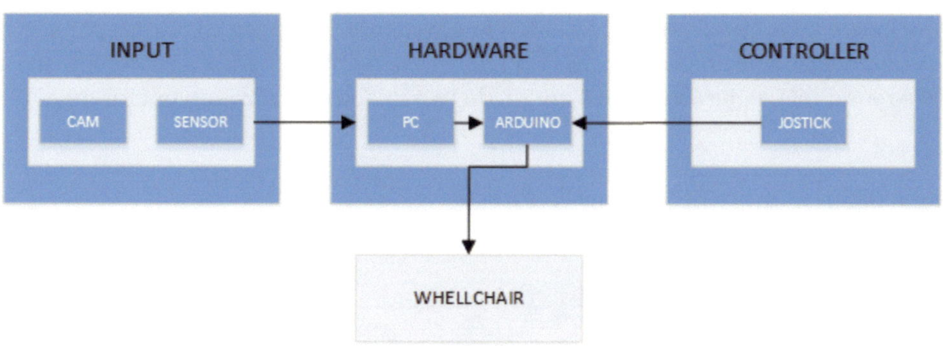

Figure 8. Chair and its embedded hardware.

A notebook with processor 1.6 GHz dual-core Intel Core i5 (Turbo Boost up to 2.7 GHz) with 3 MB and 4 GB of memory was used. The connection between the PC and the chair uses an ATmega328 microcontroller board (arduino UNO), which has 14 digital pins input/output, 6 analog inputs, and USB connection.

3.6. Architecture

The software implements the model, which seeks, from the detection of the eye status (open, closed) to inform the chair the action that should be taken especially to move forward or stop. The command "move on" triggered when the user closes his eyes unnaturally or stays with the eye closed for a period of time greater than 2 s, in about 10 frames, is analyzed, and if the detection occurs in a percentage above 90%, a command is sent, otherwise nothing is done. The command acts in a similar way as opposed to the motion to move forward as a way to clear up this script diagrammed in **Figure 9**. It was found that according to [36], the human eye takes 280 ms to blink.

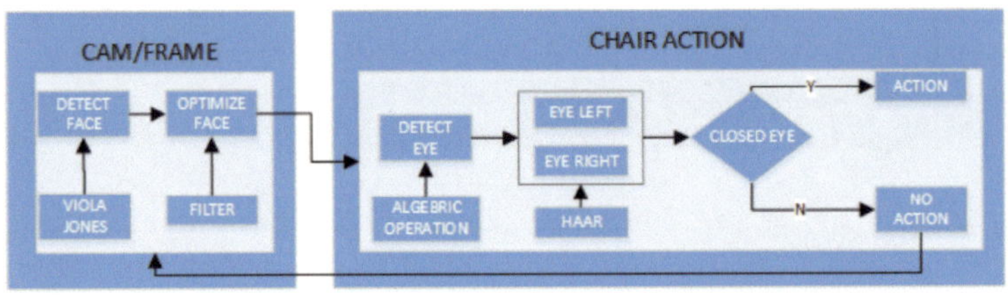

Figure 9. How to detect closed eyes.

In the proposed architecture, **Figure 9**, CAM/frame image captures through a common webcam, performs the face detection, and focuses on this area of interest; then the image is treated to minimize or neutralize lighting noise and send the information for treatment. In CHAIR ACTION, capturing is carried out prior to information and detects by means of an algebraic operation described in [36], the region where the eyes in the face are properly separated and sent to analyze the state close left eye (CL) and close right eye (CR). In the first step, the image is captured and represented in gray tones; there are 28 frames per second. In each, we use facial detector defined in [12] widely used and recognized efficiency, according to [37]. Around this region of interest are made two image optimization operations:

- Inversion;
- Retinal filter.

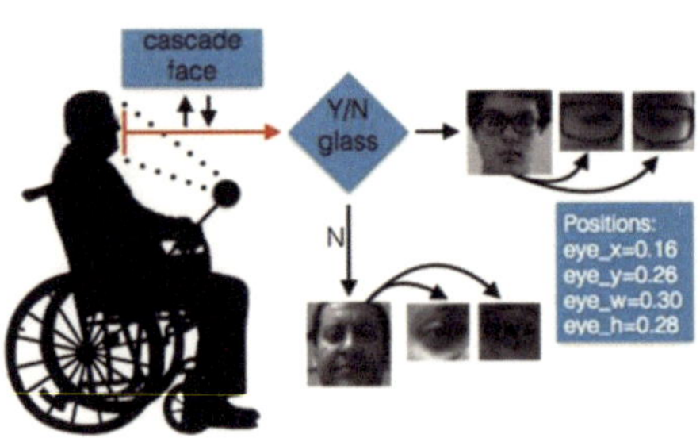

Figure 10. Eye detection structure.

Filtering through the algorithm in [38] called retinal filter cancels much of the image distortion and improves cleaning detail, even in low light (<100 lux) also keeps the naturalness. After correction of the image, an algebraic operation is made to detect the eyes of the person in the image. The completion of this step proved to be quite efficient with the use in [27] or [28] due to the fact that even after correction of the image both methods provide great instability regarding the detection of the eyes, even using different parameters as those used for the same. The extraction assumes that the person is in front of the camera and below the horizontal line of the eyes, while maintaining a fixed distance to the camera in a variable angle between **30 <** θ **< 70** as described in **Figure 10**.

3.7. Kinematic model and motion control

The kinematic model of the chair is presented as a process in which each wheel contributes both to the movement of the chair as to his/her mistake notably associated with obstacles and soil deformation. While our research ambience is indoors and appropriate to the patient, these errors can be minimized with the use of inexpensive sensors that can identify and predict possible problems in navigation.

Here we describe the mathematical idea of the chair movement that follows a traditional model of representation of the world. This model, whose movement and orientation are performed by two independent actuators, considers the rectangular object moving at speed *V*. The state plan of the chair in the Cartesian plane (*x*, *y*) is defined by the vector:

$$\left(x_c, y_c, \theta, v_c, \omega_c\right)^t \tag{2}$$

where x_c and y_c, are the coordinates of the central point of the wheel axle, Θ is the angle formed between the base of the chair $C(x_c, y_c)$, v_c is the linear velocity at the point C, and ω_c is the angular velocity,, as described in **Figure 11**.

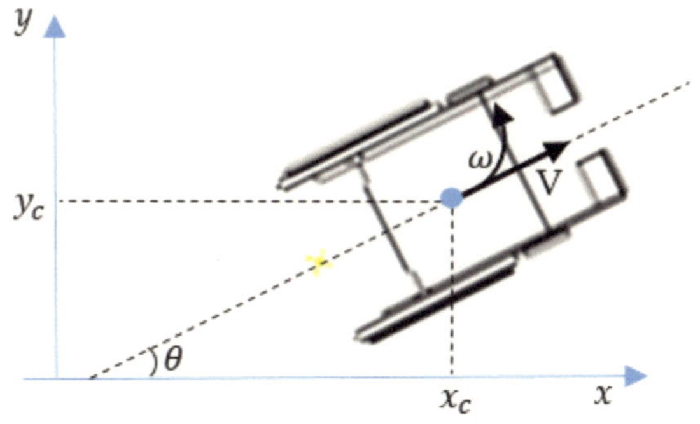

Figure 11. Cartesian representation of the chair.

The chair should move only in the direction normal to the axis of the driving wheels and can restrict the analytic relationship:

$$y'\cos\theta - x'\sin\theta \tag{3}$$

Based on the information that is obtained during the navigation, the calculation of the linear speed of each wheel is deducted for subsequent adjustment and especially in cases of unevenness through a relation between the number of pulses of the encoder N and its sampling period T.

$$v = \frac{N\pi D}{R_e T} \tag{4}$$

where v and D are, respectively, the linear velocity and the diameter of the wheel, and R_e is the encoder resolution. A possibility of representation of state variables is based on the speed at the contact point between the right wheel (v_D) and left (v_E) with the floor.

$$\left(x_c, y_c, \theta, v_D, v_E\right)^T \tag{5}$$

The choice of this form of representation is essentially the ease of mediating these quantities by odometry system.

Considering the continuous system, we have:

$$\begin{cases} v_D = \left(L + \dfrac{b}{2}\right)\omega = r_D \omega_D \\ v_E = \left(L - \dfrac{b}{2}\right)\omega = r_E \omega_E \end{cases} \tag{6}$$

Besides that

$$\begin{cases} v_D = v + \left(\dfrac{b}{2}\right)\omega \\ v_E = v - \left(\dfrac{b}{2}\right)\omega \end{cases} \tag{7}$$

Also,

$$\begin{cases} v_D + v_E = 2\omega r = 2v \\ v_D - v_E = \omega L \end{cases} \tag{8}$$

or alternatively

$$\begin{cases} v = \omega_D \dfrac{r_D}{2} + \omega_E \dfrac{r_E}{2} \\ \omega = \omega_D \dfrac{r_D}{2} + \omega_E \dfrac{r_E}{b} \end{cases} \tag{9}$$

Consider b the distance between the contact points of the wheels, r_D radius of the wheels, L the distance from point C to the center of rotation of the chair, and ω_D, ω_E, ω the angular velocities of the right, left, and center wheel movement of the chair.

From the speeds of the wheels of the robot, we may calculate the linear and angular velocities.

$$\begin{cases} v = \dfrac{v_D + v_E}{2} \\ \omega = \dfrac{v_D - v_E}{b} \end{cases} \tag{10}$$

To find out its position in the reference plane, we must know the chair state space, and how it will evolve over time with the v_D and v_E speeds.

Considering the condition called no slip can descrier the kinematic equations of motion of point C with respect to the linear (v) and angular (ω) velocity [4, 26]:

$$\begin{cases} x_c = v \cos\theta \\ y_c = v \sin\theta \\ \theta = \omega \end{cases} \tag{11}$$

or matrix form:

$$\begin{bmatrix} x_c \\ y_c \\ \theta \end{bmatrix} = \begin{bmatrix} \cos\theta & 0 \\ \sin\theta & 0 \\ 0 & 1 \end{bmatrix} \begin{bmatrix} v \\ \omega \end{bmatrix} \tag{12}$$

4. Testing and results

The performance of the closed eye detection system was built based on a set of 10,000 images of various persons. Images were acquired in a controlled lighting environment with 2048 × 1536 pixels in JPG format. For accurate detection classifier, various parameters can be changed during the training process. The influence of these parameters changes the complexity of weak classifiers, and therefore aspects as positive and false positives are influenced.

The standard size entry was set to 24 × 24 pixels. All images in our base were taken in the same, uniform background. Immediately, we wanted to see if the negative assembly constructed from the same occluded images with faces is sufficient to distinguish between open and closed eyes; using the classifier with default parameters, the following results were obtained, as described in **Figure 11**.

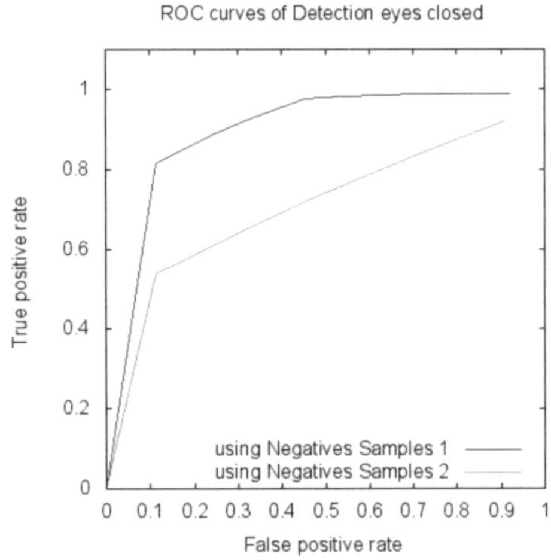

Figure 12. Comparison between detector 1 taken with random sample negatives and diverse background and using samples only performing the occlusion of the region of interest.

This analysis would serve to decrease the cost of both image search optimization and scheduling but has not proven satisfactory for such small images. Then the other negative training set was created, gathered randomly about 9000 different images that do not contain any references to human eyes. **Figure 12** shows some examples of negative training sets. As Rainer and Jochen [39] showed, the version of AdaBoost gave best results for facial detection, Gentle AdaBoost, with a ratio of false positives required cascades set to $10e^{-6}$.

http://dx.doi.org/10.5772/63816

Due to small size of the training image, we limited rectangle Haar that was used. Although the number of ways in which the rectangles may be arranged is large, for practical reasons, we limited the time with the following steps:

1. Only Haar-like with two, three, and four rectangles Was considered;
2. The size of the model of Haar features was set at a maximum of 5 × 5 and 3 × 3 pixels at least;
3. All rectangles that contribute to the unique Haar features were of the same size.

A total of 408,564 characteristic Haar were obtained by imaging under the above conditions with a satisfactory number of resources. For this problem, four detectors were used which were constructed and differed primarily by the type of boost used and parameter variation as described in **Table 2**, wherein MinHitRate is the minimum hit rate desired for each phase of the classifier; MaxFalseAlarm is the maximum false alarm rate desired for each phase of the classifier; Nstages is the number of cascaded stages; BTYPE is the kind of boost used (type of boosted classifiers: DAB— Discrete AdaBoost, RAB—Real AdaBoost, LB—LogitBoost, GAB—Gentle AdaBoost); WTRate is the cutting line and the weight used in the boost; and Wcout is the maximum count of false trees for all stages of the cascade.

Parameter	Sorter 1	Sorter 2	Sorter 3	Sorter 4
MinHitRate	0.9–0.999	0.9–0.999	0.9–0.999	0.9–0.999
MaxFalseAlarm	0.1–0.5	0.1–0.5	0.1–0.5	0.1–0.5
Nstages	20	25	20	25
Btype	GAB	RAB	LB	DAB
WTRate	0.95–0.98	0.95–0.98	0.95–0.98	0.95–0.98
Wcount	100	100	100	100

Table 2. Presentation of parameters and classifiers.

As shown in **Figure 13**, the results are established with great parameter, and the results are described in **Table 3**.

Figure 13. Negative sample.

Parameter	Sorter 1	Sorter 2	Sorter 3	Sorter 4
MinHitRate	0.999	0.987	0.985	0.999
MaxFalseAlarm	0.5	0.5	0.4	0.5
Nstages	20	25	20	25
Btype	GAB	RAB	LB	DAB
WTRate	0.97	0.98	0.95	0.95
Wcount	100	100	100	100
Processing time	4 days	5 days	4 days	7 days

Table 3. Presentation of results and better processing time.

Figure 14 shows the difference between the result of the public detector and the detector with better response. Both have a good recognition rate, but positive for higher rates against false positives makes the classifier "olhosfechadosGAB" provide better performance.

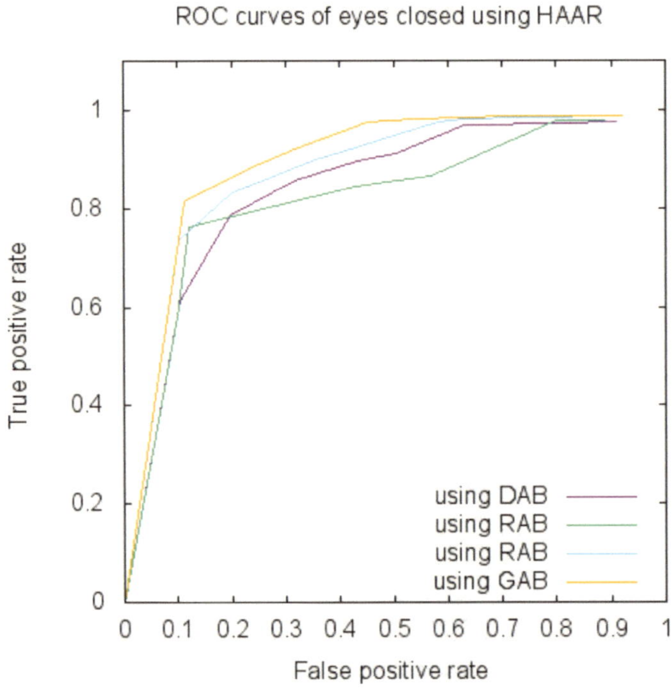

Figure 14. ROC graph with the best parameters and analysis for different versions of AdaBoost.

Simulating what will happen directly in the chair is crucial. Therefore there were two tests: the first with 12 volunteers, conducted during the same period of time (2 min) recording a video with one's image of the front face held at specified times to opening and closing the eyes, with the following results described in **Figure 15**.

http://dx.doi.org/10.5772/63816

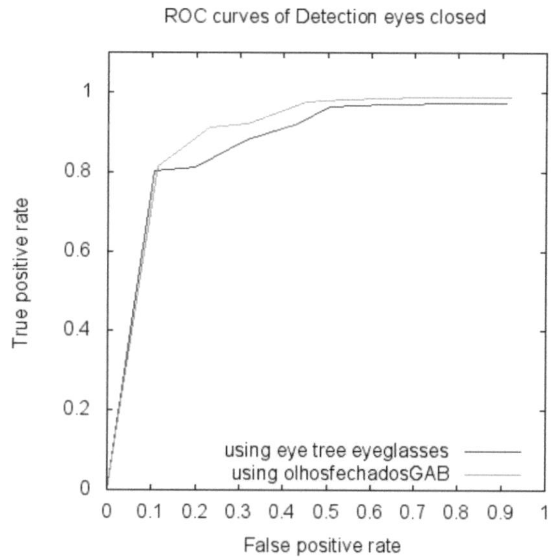

Figure 15. Comparison of our classifier and public distribution.

In the second test, the same group of volunteers held navigation CD from point A to point B, which would use a region of 1 square meter stopping place, as shown in **Figure 16**.

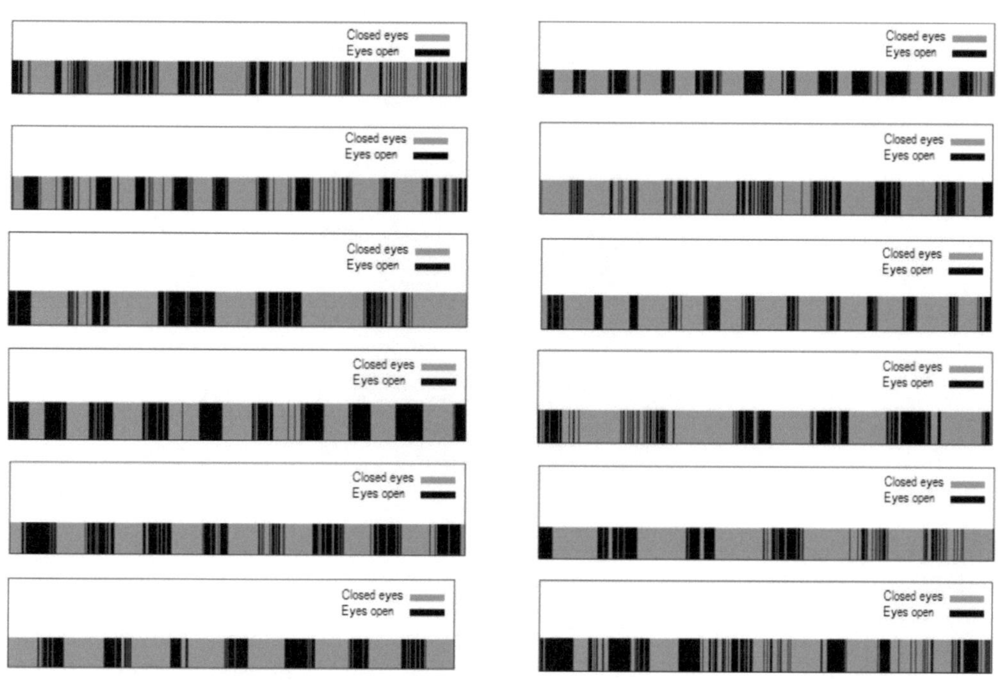

Figure 16. Result detection of volunteers.

Volunteers can perform spins of the head that do not exceed 30 degrees, in an environment with good lighting conditions (above 200 lux). In carrying out the detection was operated with frame size 640 by 320 with 28 FPS. In all, the volunteers were able to make the journey without difficulty with stopped or early movement. During the test, we observed the total time hardware response to commands, and these times ranged from 250 to 300 ms.

5. Conclusion

The tests clearly demonstrated that HCC can be successfully used in a blink detection system, and the combination of the classifier set to closed eyes and face resulted in a fast and efficient system.

The trained detector (one classifier) with the parameters described in **Table 2** exceeded the detector OpenCV framework proposed by both the rate of detection and computational efficiency. In this study, we were able to detect approximately 98% of the results with about 9% false positives.

The results showed that the use of regionalized data enables more efficient detection. We observed that the detector does not fail to be submitted to the people with whom he/she was trained. To set a robust system, the patient must have a face image trained classifier with a significant number of possessions.

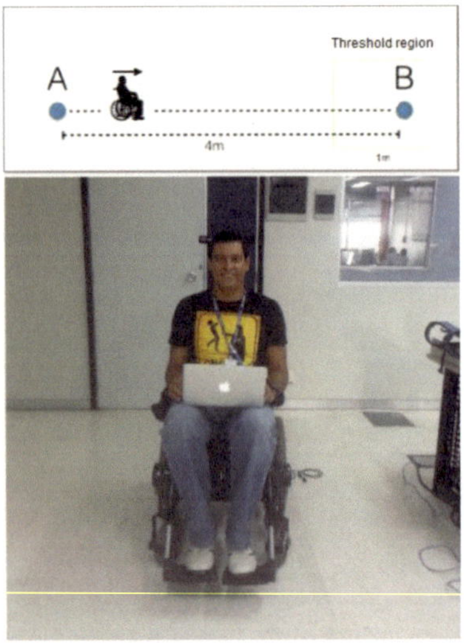

Figure 17. Conducted in chair.

The average error was 0.058, while applying the minimum neighboring detector returned a number of 90% positive, while for the maximum number of neighbors obtained 98% as detection windows scan across the image with the maximum neighboring the intersection between the windows is unique and therefore there is no possibility of true or false.

http://dx.doi.org/10.5772/63816

Another crucial point is the detector oscillation while the individual closes and opens his eyes. This set of errors stabilizes in a few milliseconds (would not be a problem if this time (**Figure 17**) did not result in "leaps" in the chair). The solution to this problem was given by using a waiting time for stabilization of detection (about 1 s), and thereafter the chair had its start and stop smoothly performed.

Using our PC, it was possible to obtain an average rate of 280 ms detector response, and the architecture proved to be quite stable, no crash or time-consuming to user responses. Individuals engaged in the work reported that it would not require extensive training to use the chair and (after 30 min of test) and did not experience discomfort when using the system (**Figure 18**).

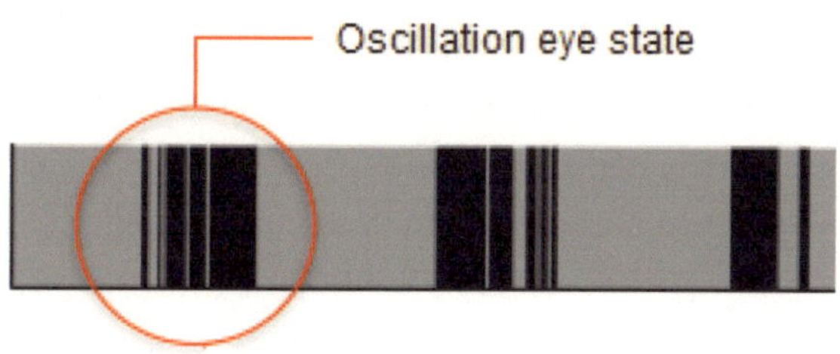

Figure 18. Detector response analysis.

As future work, we highlight the implementation of the navigation control with the head that will allow the user to perform turns and spins with the chair and the analysis of all these ideas applied to a larger architecture and its integration with other low-cost sensors that allow to bypass obstacles.

Author details

Marcos Figueredo[1*], Alexandre Nascimento[2], Roberto L.S. Monteiro[1,3] and Marcelo A. Moret[3,4]

*Address all correspondence to: mbfigueredo@uneb.br

1 Department of Exact Sciences and Earth—DECET II, College of Information Systems—Alagoinhas, State University of Bahia—UNEB, Bahia, Brazil

2 College ÁREA1, Salvador, Bahia, Brazil

3 Doctoral Program in Computational Modeling and Industrial Technology, College of SENAI-CIMATEC Technology, Salvador, Bahia, Brazil

4 Department of Exact Sciences and Earth—DCET, Campus I, State University of Feira de Santana—UESF, Salvador, Bahia, Brazil

References

[1] Instituto Brasileiro de Geografia e Estatística—IBGE. Características da população e dos domicílios resultados do universo, Censo Demográfico 2010, vol. 1, p. 161, 2011.

[2] BRAGA, Rodrigo António Marques et al. Plataforma de desenvolvimento de cadeiras de rodas inteligentes. PhD, Thesis, Faculty of Engineering, University of Puerto, PhD Program in Computer Science, Porto, Portugal, set 2012.

[3] HALAWANI, Alaa et al. Active vision for controlling an electric wheelchair. Intelligent Service Robotics, v. 5, n. 2, pp. 89–98, 2012.

[4] SONG, You; LUO, Yunfeng; LIN, Jun. Detection of movements of head and mouth to provide computer access for disabled. In: 2011 International Conference on Technologies and Applications of Artificial Intelligence (TAAI). IEEE, 2011, pp. 223–226.

[5] ZHAO, Zheng; WANG, Yuchuan; FU, Shengbo. Head movement recognition based on Lucas-Kanade algorithm. In: 2012 International Conference on Computer Science & Service System (CSSS). IEEE, 2012, pp. 2303–2306.

[6] RUMÃO DE MELO, Valdenice. Avaliação da qualidade de vida de pacientes com lesão medular acompanhados em regime ambulatorial. Master's thesis - Federal University of Pernambuco. CCS. Neuropsychiatry and Behavioral Sciences, 2009.

[7] CEZAR DA CRUZ, Daniel Marinho; AUGUSTO IOSHIMOTO, Maria Teresa. Tecnologia assistiva para as atividades de vida diária na tetraplegia completa c6 pós-lesão medular. Magazine Triângulo, v. 3, n. 2, 2011.

[8] Learning OPENCV. Computer vision with the OpenCV library. GaryBradski & Adrian Kaebler. O'Reilly, 2008.

[9] BRAGA, Rodrigo António Marques et al. Concept and design of the intellwheels platform for developing intelligent wheelchairs. In: Informatics in Control, Automation and Robotics, Springer-Verlag, Berlin Heidelberg, 2009, pp. 191–203.

[10] JIAN-ZHENG, Liu; ZHENG, Zhao. Head movement recognition based on lk algorithm and gentleboost. In: 2011 7th International Conference on Networked Computing and Advanced Information Management (NCM). IEEE, 2011, pp. 232–236.

[11] JOLLIFFE, Ian. Principal Component Analysis. John Wiley & Sons, Ltd, 2002.

[12] VIOLA, Paul; JONES, Michael. Rapid object detection using a boosted cascade of simple features. In: Proceedings of the 2001 IEEE Computer Society Conference on Computer Vision and Pattern Recognition, 2001. CVPR 2001. IEEE, 2001, 1, pp. I-511–I-518.

[13] DYMOND, Elizabeth; POTTER, Roger. Head movements for control of assistive technology. Engineering in Medicine and Biology Society. In: 14th Annual International Conference of the IEEE, 1992, 4, pp. 1527–1528.

[14] BASU, Sumit; ESSA, Irfan; PENTLAND, Alex. Motion regularization for model-based head tracking. In: Proceedings of the IEEE International Conference on Pattern Recognition (ICPR '96). Vienna, Austria, 1996, 3, pp. 611–616.

[15] KIRULUTA, Andrew; EIZENMAN, Moshe; PASUPATHY, Subbarayan. Predictive head movement tracking using a Kalman filter. IEEE Transactions on Systems, Man, and Cybernetics—Part B: Cybernetics, v. 27, n. 2, pp. 326–331, 1997.

[16] TAYLOR, P. B.; NGUYEN, H. T. Performance of a head-movement interface for wheelchair control. In: Proceedings of the 25" Annual International Conference of the IEEE EMBS, 2003, pp. 17–21.

[17] NGUYEN, H. T.; KING, L. M.; KNIGHT, G. Real-time head movement system and embedded linux implementation for the control of power wheelchairs. In: 26th Annual International Conference of the IEEE Engineering in Medicine and Biology Society, 2004. IEMBS'04. IEEE, 2004, pp. 4892–4895.

[18] LIAO, Wei-Kai; COHEN, Isaac. Classifying facial gestures in presence of head motion computer vision and pattern recognition – workshops. IEEE Computer Society Conference on CVPR Workshops. 2005, p. 77.

[19] MANOGNA, S.; VAISHNAVI, Sree; GEETHANJALI, B. Head movement based assist system for physically challenged. In: 4th International Conference on Bioinformatics and Biomedical Engineering (iCBBE), 2010, pp. 1–4.

[20] WEI, L.; HU, H.; LU, T. & YUAN, K. Evaluating the performance of a face movement based wheelchair control interface in an indoor environment. In: Proceedings of the IEEE International Conference on Robotics and Biomimetics, 2010, pp. 387–392.

[21] LEE, Chan-Su; SAMARAS, Dimitris. Analysis and synthesis of facial expressions using decomposable nonlinear generative models. In: 2011 IEEE International Conference on Automatic Face & Gesture Recognition and Workshops (FG 2011). IEEE, 2011, pp. 847–852.

[22] ERIKSSON, Martin; PAPANIKOTOPOULOS, Nikolaos P. Eye-tracking for detection of driver fatigue. In: IEEE Conference on Intelligent Transportation System, 1997. ITSC'97. IEEE, 1997, pp. 314–319.

[23] ERIKSSON, Martin; PAPANIKOLOPOULOS, Nikolaos P. Driver fatigue: a vision-based approach to automatic diagnosis. Transportation Research Part C: Emerging Technologies, v. 9, n. 6, pp. 399–413, 2001.

[24] LIN, Chern-Sheng; CHANG, Kai-Chieh; JAIN, Young-Jou. A new data processing and calibration method for an eye-tracking device pronunciation system. Optics & Laser Technology, v. 34, n. 5, pp. 405–413, 2002.

[25] JI, Qiang; YANG, Xiaojie. Real-time eye, gaze, and face pose tracking for monitoring driver vigilance. Real-Time Imaging, v. 8, n. 5, pp. 357–377, 2002.

[26] ARAI, Kohei; MARDIYANTO, Ronny. Eyes based electric wheel chair control system. International Journal of Advanced Computer Science and Applications, v. 2, n. 12, 2011.

[27] CHAU, Michael; BETKE, Margrit. Real time eye tracking and blink detection with USB cameras. Boston University Computer Science, v. 2215, n. 2005–2012, pp. 1–10, 2005.

[28] FAZLI, Saeid; ESFEHANI, Parisa. Tracking eye state for fatigue detection. In: International Conference on Advances in Computer and Electrical Engineering (ICACEE 2012). 2012. pp. 17–20.

[29] ALSHAQAQI, Belal et al. Driver drowsiness detection system. In: 2013 8th International Workshop on Systems, Signal Processing and their Applications (WoSSPA). IEEE, 2013, pp. 151–155.

[30] SAINI, Vandna; SAINI, Rekha. Driver drowsiness detection system and techniques: a review. International Journal of Computer Science and Information Technologies, v. 5, n. 3, pp. 4245–4249, 2014.

[31] HJELMÅS, Erik; LOW, Boon Kee. Face detection: a survey. Computer Vision and Image Undertanding, v. 83, n. 3, pp. 236–274, 2001.

[32] SCHAPIRE, Robert E. The strength of weak learnability. Machine Learning, v. 5, n. 2, pp. 197–227, 1990.

[33] NOCK, Richard; NIELSEN, Frank. A real generalization of discrete adaboost. Frontiers in Artificial Intelligence and Applications, v. 141, p. 509, 2006.

[34] GAO, Wei; ZHOU, Zhi-Hua. Approximation stability and boosting. Algorithmic Learning Theory, v. 21, pp. 59–73, 2010.

[35] HORTON, Michael; CAMERON-JONES, Mike; WILLIAMS, Raymond. Multiple classifier object detection with confidence measures. In: AI 2007: Advances in Artificial Intelligence. Springer, Berlin, Heidelberg, 2007, pp. 559–568.

[36] EKMAN, Paul; ROSENBERG, Erika L. What the face reveals: Basic and applied studies of spontaneous expression using the Facial Action Coding System (FACS). Oxford University Press, USA, 1997.

[37] TURK, Matthew; PENTLAND, Alex. Eigenfaces for recognition. Journal of Cognitive Neuroscience, v. 3, n. 1, pp. 71–86, 1991.

[38] BENOIT, Alexandre et al. Using human visual system modeling for bio-inspired low level image processing. Computer Vision and Image Understanding, v. 114, n. 7, pp. 758–773, 2010.

[39] LIENHART, Rainer; MAYDT, Jochen. An extended set of haar-like features for rapid object detection. In: Proceedings of the 2002 International Conference on Image Processing. IEEE, 2002. pp. I-900–I-903, vol. 1.

Chapter 6

Watch Your Step! Terrain Traversability for Robot Control

Mauro Bellone

Additional information is available at the end of the chapter

http://dx.doi.org/10.5772/64489

Abstract

Watch your step! Or perhaps, watch your wheels. Whatever the robot is, if it puts its feet, tracks, or wheels in the wrong place, it might get hurt; and as robots are quickly going from structured and completely known environments towards uncertain and unknown terrain, the surface assessment becomes an essential requirement. As a result, future mobile robots cannot neglect the evaluation of terrain's structure, according to their driving capabilities. With the objective of filling this gap, the focus of this study was laid on terrain analysis methods, which can be used for robot control with particular reference to autonomous vehicles and mobile robots. Giving an overview of theory related to this topic, the investigation not only covers hardware, such as visual sensors or laser scanners, but also space descriptions, such as digital elevation models and point descriptors, introducing new aspects and characterization of terrain assessment. During the discussion, a wide number of examples and methodologies are exposed according to different tools and sensors, including the description of a recent method of terrain assessment using normal vectors analysis. Indeed, normal vectors has demonstrated great potentialities in the field of terrain irregularity assessment in both on-road and off-road environments.

Keywords: traversability, terrain assessment, terrain analysis, UGV, mobile robots

1. Introduction

From an analysis in the United States, the automated guided vehicles (AGVs) market will be worth 2240 million dollars by 2020, due to growing automation investments across all major industries [1]. Besides, BI Intelligence estimates a number of 10 million cars and trucks featuring self-driving capabilities by the same year [2]. On the other side, during the DARPA Robotics Challenge 2015, worldwide universities and their humanoids have raced among challenging scenarios, and a number of robots lost their balance traveling across rubble [3], and some of them even used semi-autonomous systems to overcome this challenge by manually sending commands about specific locations where to put their feet on. Additionally, the Curiosity rover, recently sent on Mars by NASA, demonstrates the growing utilization of robotics technologies in planetary exploration as they require high level of reliability during their surveys, and rocks or terrain irregularities may cause irreparable damages to on-board instrumentation [4].

The common element among all these types of robots consists of the necessity of a high level of driving capability; though motion control has made great strides, it may fail in case of unexpected circumstances, including road hazards, pavement distresses, and rubble. As a result, from widely known AGVs, spread in industries since years, to modern unmanned ground vehicles (UGVs) [5], the high level of driving capabilities is perceived an essential requirement. In order to enhance robustness and reliability, future mobile robots should be designed including custom hardware and software components, helping UGVs to adapt their driving behavior according to surface irregularities. In robotics, the assessment of terrain conditions is generally referred to as *"terrain traversability analysis;"* even though traversability has been explored from various perspectives, a thorough survey on this topic suggests that a specific definition is still missing in the robotic community [6]. On the other hand, as robots' diffusion increases braking up new boundaries in their application, the use of visual technologies for traversability assessment will improve their reliability; consequently, the acquisition of information about the terrain is a prerequisite capacity and recent advances in sensors and perception encourage future researched in this field.

Among the number of methods and models for terrain analysis, there are at least two large categories, (i) *classification-based* methods and (ii) *cost-assessment* methods. In the former, it is possible to count all the approaches that consider a binary distinction of the terrain as two classes, traversable or non-traversable; to cite an example, in [7], the authors use an on-line trained classifier to distinguish traversable and non-traversable regions. Widely spread in research, occupancy maps also fall in this category as they use the elevation of surrounding objects to construct a map of occupied regions on the base of sensor measurements [8]. Whereas in cost-assessment methods is common to assign a continuous cost index, to better describe the traversability characteristics of terrain according to a specific cost function [9]. As advances on the same line, Tanaka et al. implemented a fuzzy-based traversability analysis, considering terrain roughness and slope as input for a fuzzy inference system and then generating a vector field histogram for navigation purposes [10].

A further classification of methods commonly used in this field distinguishes between *geometric-* or *appearance-based* methods. Used in a large number of works in research [11–13], geometric-based analyses aim to detect traversability using geometric properties of surfaces such as distances in space and shapes. Whereas appearance methods, to a greater extent related to camera images processing and cognitive analyses, have the objective of recognize colors and patterns not related to the common appearance of terrain, such as grass, rocks or vegetation [14, 15]. In spite of the clear potentialities of appearance-based methods, still geometric ones are mostly common in robotics, because they can be easily used for path-planning purposes, where also probabilistic methods are gaining interest. Indeed, in 2006, Thrun et al. [16]

presented a probabilistic algorithm for terrain classification on a fast moving robot platform, constituting a part of their autonomous vehicle during the Darpa Grand Challenge in 2005. As a recent example, in [17], the authors describe a terrain classification approach for an autonomous robot based on Markov random fields (MRFs) on fused 3D laser and camera image data.

In the light of glaring requirements of terrain analysis for future UGVs, this discussion aims at exploring some of the basic concepts of traversability; the focus was laid on geometric methods. This study introduces a definition of traversability and its application to robot control and autonomous ground vehicles. This directly leads to the contributions of this chapter, which attempts to compare different methodologies and fill the gap between theory and practical applications giving a definition that can be of general value for terrain traversability analysis in terms of a fuzzy set, including practical examples to foregoing functions available in the literature. Furthermore, the potentialities of novel methods based on the normal vectors analysis will be explored, providing some practical examples of application.

The chapter is structured as follow: Section 2 will provide an overview and basic knowledge about the field with focus on related works and recent techniques for visual terrain analysis, used sensors and space representation. Later, in Section 3, a theoretical background will help, who unfamiliar with the topic, to understand the basic concepts related to robot models and state spaces, introducing a definition of traversability in terms of a fuzzy set. Examples, results and comparisons are exposed during a thorough discussion in Section 4, which will cover basic functions and recent researches in the field applied on both synthetic data and real scenarios. Conclusions are drawn in Section 5.

2. Overview

As humans themselves rely on their five senses to know where to walk or drive a vehicle on, creating an implicit space representation in the brain, robots perceive and interpret the space using exteroceptive and proprioceptive transducers as a sensing aid. In order to build an effective exteroceptive traversability analysis tool two elements are required: (i) visual sensors and (ii) a mathematical space representation. The former comprises any exteroceptive sensor such as cameras, depth cameras, or time-of-flight sensors, which endow robots with sensing capabilities; whereas the latter provides a spatial organization of sensory data and build an abstract representation of the 3D environment. As a result, the approach to terrain traversability analysis may change according to space representation, as much as the available data may vary according to the type of sensor. Even though the most common methods for terrain traversability analysis are based on exteroceptive perception [9], for the sake of completeness, it is important to cite that proprioceptive sensors are also successfully used for terrain analysis [18–20], measuring and interpreting quantities such as vibrations or slippage, but their study is out of the scope of this study.

To facilitate the comprehension of the content of this discussion, following a short review on space representations and sensor technologies available for terrain analysis in mobile robotics is reported.

2.1. Sensors for terrain analysis

Sensing denotes a group of techniques used in robotics to measure any physical quantity interacting with the robot. Hence, any device used to acquire information can be counted in this category. Although the general concept of sensing as the problem of understanding how a robot see the world, by means of a set of visual sensors, has been addressed following various approaches, in the specific topic of traversability, there are a number of open issues still to be solved. In [21], the author has accurately described the problem of semantic perception for a robot operating in human-living environments, approaching the problem from sensors and data point of view. Notwithstanding the valuable work done in the field of perception, the indoor structured environments introduce a number of simplifications which are never applicable in outdoor unstructured environments. First of all, indoor scenarios are generally characterized by smooth ground surfaces and high-size objects represented as vertical planes. For this reason, AGVs, commonly used in indoor industrial environments, do not consider any terrain representation at all. Moreover, indoor robots generally move at low speed, and consequently, they do not require any sophisticated system for terrain analysis. The situation changes totally in the case of planetary rovers [4], driving on sandy terrains featuring rocks, varying in size and shape. Furthermore, recent driverless cars are quickly going towards public roads; in such situations, rocks, road hazards, and pavement distresses may put the vehicle, and its passengers, in serious danger [22].

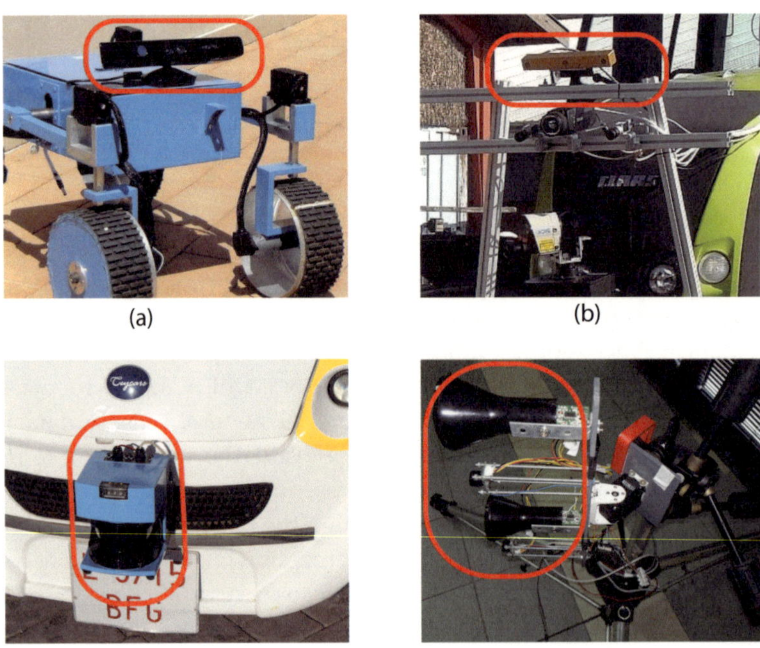

Figure 1. Examples of sensing devices in which: (a) is a depth camera, the Kinect sensor, mounted on an experimental planetary rover, (b) is a stereovision system including the XB3 Bumblebee camera used on an agricultural tractor, in (c) an autonomous electric car featuring a Sick laser, and (d) is an ultrasonic sensor-based mechatronic device.

http://dx.doi.org/10.5772/64489

Since this discussion examines terrain analysis, a distinction between acquisition and representation of information should be done. On one hand, the space acquisition strongly depends on the typology of sensors and applications; on the other hand, its representation depends on the perception meaning and its content. From a purely geometrical point of view, the most primitive representation of a point in the space is the 3D Euclidean metric. However, the information about the real 3D coordinates of a specific point can be obtained by triangulation techniques [23, 24] on stereocamera images, or by directly measuring its distance using time-of-flight (TOF) systems [25]. **Figure 1** shows typical image sensors assembled on several UGVs in order to acquire some of the images used for the experimental discussion in this work. Specifically, **Figure 1a** depicts a depth sensor, the Kinect camera, used in [26] for a novel approach to terrain analysis, whereas in **Figure 1b** a more sophisticated vision system designed for an agricultural tractor is shown [27], the red circle marks a trinocular stereocamera. **Figure 1c** and **Figure 1d** show two examples of time-of-flight sensors, a Sick laser range finder and a sonar sensing system. Following, the technology at the base of such sensors will be briefly recalled.

2.1.1. Stereovision

Stereocameras constitute a family of cameras composed by two or more lenses with separated image sensors. They provide a visual image for each lens and post-elaboration attempts to estimate the distance of each point from the sensor by means of connections between correspondences seen by two different lenses at the same time, simulating the human binocular vision. In order to provide accurate measures, the sensors require the perfect calibration with respect to each other, done by the extrapolation of their intrinsic and extrinsic parameters.

In the literature, a large number of methods for camera calibration are available. As an example, Kearney et al. propose a method for the calibration using geometric constraints in [28] and then Puget and Skordas present a method for optimizing the calibration [29]. Later, many researchers studied methods for fast and accurate calibration of multiple cameras [30], in anticipation of the most recent researches of automatic calibration for cars, for example [31]. Recent sensors use more than two cameras for the triangulation in order to increase the accuracy in both short and long range. The 3D representation of the environment is inferred detecting the same point into both camera images, and the bigger the set of points the richer will be the 3D space reconstruction.

Simplifying the concept, said d the distance from a point p measured by a binocular stereocamera, then:

$$d = \frac{fb}{\| x_1 - x_2 \|}, \tag{1}$$

where f is the focal distance of the sensors, b is the baseline, that is, the spacing between the sensors, and x_1, x_2 are the coordinates of p in the two images expressed in terms of pixels.

An example of a trinocular camera featuring multiple baseline can be seen in **Figure 1b**, where the sensor has been mounted as visual aid on an experimental tractor [27].

2.1.2. Time-of-flight 3D sensors

In contrast to stereocameras, TOF-based systems, such as lasers and sonars, directly evaluate distances by the measurement of the delay until an emitted signal hits a surface and returns back to the receiver, thus estimating the true distance from the sensor to the surface. Also in this case, a simplified relation can calculate the distance between the sensor and a point in the space as follows:

$$d = \frac{ct}{2}, \tag{2}$$

where c is the speed of the ray, light in case of lasers, and t is the amount of time since the emission until the reception. However, in case of ultrasonic sensors, the speed of the ray depends of its wavelength and the estimation of the distance as well as the localization problem become harder due to the wider beam which may be cause of multiple reflections. As an example, in [32], the authors propose three different mathematical approaches to detect position and orientation of an observer, such as a robot, with respect to a smooth surface. Such ultrasonic-based system is depicted in **Figure 1d**. In contrast to ultrasonic technology, laser scanners are much more precises and reliables for environment description. To underline the global diffusion of laser scanners, **Figure 1c** shows a Sick 3D laser range finder applied on an electric autonomous vehicle at University of Almería (Spain) [33]. As proof of the higher performance of lasers, Borrmann et al. obtained an accurate space description from a laser scanner and use laser information to build a global map in outdoor urban environment [34]. Besides this research, a large number of scientists continuously propose new methods for the 3D space reconstruction using 3D laser scanner technologies.

Thanks to their properties of accuracy and reliability, the research involving vision for mobile robot shifted towards the use of laser technologies as an aid for space reconstruction.

2.2. Space representations

The term *space representation* roboticists refer to an abstract depiction of robots' surrounding environment. As robots live in the three-dimensional space, the most natural space representation should be the Euclidean 3D space, but handling 3D space data may be hard and time-consuming. Thus, for computational performance purposes, the most used foregoing space representation has been the $2\frac{1}{2}$-dimensional, such as digital elevation models (DEM) better described later in this section. Only recently, thanks to the high performing CPU and GPUs, 3D point descriptors are gaining interest in this field.

http://dx.doi.org/10.5772/64489

2.2.1. *Digital elevation maps*

Organizing sensors data is a mandatory step to reconstruct information for geometric interpretation purposes, and digital elevation models (DEM) [35] are widely used as space representation in mobile robotics. Although topography and large areas terrain mapping constitute the original use of DEMs, their use for traversability analysis has been demonstrated as successful in mobile robotics [4]. As further example, Larson et al. discuss a real-time approach to analyze the traversability of off-road terrain for UGVs considering positive and negative obstacles through elevation information [36].

DEMs have been introduced as a compact $2\frac{1}{2}$-dimensional representation, which assumes that a surface can be represented as an elevation function $g(x,y), g: \mathbb{R}^2 \rightarrow \mathbb{R}$, where x and y are the coordinates on a regularly sampled plane. As a result, a grid-based space representation is obtained, in which a surface is described by a finite number of points collected in a fixed size grid structure. **Figure 2** shows an example of a DEM representation obtained from a stereo-camera images, the entire procedure shows the process from a camera image, see **Figure 2a**, to point cloud in **Figure 2b**, and DEM, **Figure 2c**. Though compact the DEM representation requires a further step from acquisition to 3D reconstruction and DEM generation, whereas working on purely 3D data implies that one step can be skipped.

Figure 2. Example of two different space representations in which (b) is a point cloud representation, whereas (c) is the relative DEM, both geometrically describing the scene in the camera image (a).

The classical DEM approach constitutes an efficient representation, but it lacks of accuracy in space description since objects are described as surfaces using their elevation without taking into account their real shape. For instance, a tunnel cannot be represented using a digital elevation model. As an improvement of classical DEMs approach, Pfaff et al. [37] proposed the extended DEMs or the so-called *extended elevation maps* (EEM). Such technique involves the use of additional information in order to have a better description of objects and space; furthermore, the authors also used a Kalman filter to enhance the terrain description in a DEM taking into account measurements error and uncertainties. Recently, in [38], the researchers used EEM as multilayer digital maps for the description of volcano areas.

In conclusion, though suitable due to its compactness and simplicity, in each DEM formalization, there is the assumption of regularity in the surface and it turns into a not-complete space representation. As the matter of fact, it fails in a large number of practical situations; nevertheless, it is extensively used in robotics since it is simply applicable in low-performance embedded controllers.

2.2.2. Point descriptors

A recent space description, used in robotics for traversability purposes, consists in the representation of each point simply by its 3D Cartesian coordinates [24]. Hence, let us define a *point cloud* as a set of scattered 3D points, that is:

$$\mathcal{P} = \left\{ p_i \left(x_i, y_i, z_i \right) \in \mathbb{R}^3, i = 1, 2, \ldots, n, n \in \mathbb{N} \right\}, \tag{3}$$

where n is the number of elements in the set. In order to provide a coherent space representation, the coordinates of each point $p_i \in \mathcal{P}$ have to be given respect to a common coordinate system. The origin of such reference frame is usually located into the robot's geometric center or the sensing device, defined as camera reference frame $RF_c(O_c, x_c, y_c, z_c)$. For this reason, generally distance data need an additional coordinate transformation using appropriate rotation matrices. As a result, 3D space description in form as point cloud constitutes a simple and robust solution to represent environments for robotic purposes. In the most recent data representation, the RGB color information is added to points obtaining the so-called RGB-D point clouds. As an example, **Figure 2b** shows an RGB-D point cloud obtained as triangulation of stereopairs in outdoor road environment. Nowadays, it is common to think the 3D points as defined in the three-dimensional meaning of Euclidean metric and represented by its Cartesian coordinates (x, y, z). However, problems such as perception and recognition in point clouds are ill-posed, if only the geometric coordinates of points are considered. In spite of the addition of new characteristics of points, such as color or intensity, may help, the problem remains ill-posed due to the ambiguity of matching between points. In particular, a point in a cloud can be seen as a single point, yet it could represent the intersection of perpendicular planes representing the sides of an object, and therefore, it could be described using semantic meanings such as "vertex" or "edge." The set of characteristics used to describe a point defines a *local descriptor.* As a result, in the context of perception, the concept of 3D point as described only by its coordinates is substituted by the concept of local descriptor.

Let be given a point cloud $\mathcal{P}$, defined as in Eq. (3), and let us consider a point p_q the so-called *query point,* the neighborhood of p_q in $\mathcal{P}$ can be defined as the set of points such that:

$$P^q = \left\{p_i \in \mathcal{P} \subset \mathbb{R}^3 : \left|p_i - p^q\right| \le d_m \forall i = 1,2,\dots,k\right\}, \tag{4}$$

where d_m, the so-defined as *search radius,* is the maximum distance between p^q and each neighbor, k is the number of neighbors of p^q in P^q, and $|\cdot|$ is a generic norm (without loss of generality, it is possible to refer to the Euclidean distance).

A local descriptor of p_q can be defined as the vector function F that describes the information content of P^d according to a specific characteristic:

$$F\left(p^q, P^q\right) = \left\{x_1^q, x_2^q, \dots, x_n^q\right\}, \tag{5}$$

where x_i^q is the *ith* dimension of the descriptor. By comparing the local descriptors of two points, namely p_1 and p_2, it is possible to estimate their differences. Let Γ be the measure of similarity between p_1 and p_2, with their associated descriptors F_1 and F_2, and let d be their distance:

$$\Gamma = d\left(F_1, F_2\right). \tag{6}$$

Then, d is a scalar function and can be considered as the degree of similarity between points. If $\Gamma \to 0$ two points can be considered similar according to the specific characteristics set. Conversely, if Γ increases the points will have different properties. It is important to note that the effectiveness of the explicit expression of descriptors is given by its ability to differentiate points in the presence of rigid transformations, noise, sampling variations, changes in scale, or illumination. Moreover, the generality of the representation of points using descriptors allows to collect points and their characteristics such as color, but also traversability, as a vector in the form of a point cloud.

A possible application of point clouds for traversability analysis can be found in [14], where the authors describe a method for terrain classification using point clouds data obtained by stereovision. They propose the use of superpixels as the visual primitives for traversability estimation using a learning algorithm. A different approach can be found in [39]; here, the authors acquire information about terrain by a LIDAR and, using local 3D point statistics, segment it into three classes: clutter to capture grass and tree canopy, linear to capture thin objects such as wires or tree branches, and finally surface to capture solid objects such as ground terrain surface, rocks or tree trunks. As further example, in [40], the authors use a Sick lidar to acquire point cloud and build a traversability cost-to-go function for navigation purposes.

2.2.3. *A comparison among methods for terrain analysis*

To finalize this overview, it is worth to compare different methods according to their use in the scientific community and provide a classification of the used approaches. **Table 1** presents a summary of references in the field of terrain analysis and traversability, classifying them for space representation and used sensor, the full bullet indicates the classification. More specifically, the classification of used sensors distinguishes between ToF and stereocameras as method to acquire information, whereas the space description classification differentiates between DEMs and point clouds, including in the last category also point descriptors.

Reference	**Application**	**Sensors** **ToF I Stereo**	**Space representation** **DEM I Pt.C**
Bellone et al. [27]	Natural	● I ●	○ I ●
Bellone and Reina [41]	Automotive	● I ○	○ I ●
Braun et al. [42]	Natural	○ I ●	● I ○
Broggi et al. [13]	Automotive	○ I ●	● I ○
Cafaro et al. [43]	Search and rescue	● I ○	○ I ●
Dargazanv and Berns [44]	Natural	○ I ●	○ I ●
Dongshin et al. [14]	Natural	○ I ●	○ I ●
Haselich et al. [17]	Natural	● I ○	● I ○
Ishigami et al. [45]	Planetary	● I ○	● I ○
Kubota et al. [46]	Planetary	● I ○	● I ○
Larson et al. [36]	Natural	● I ○	● I ○
Neuhus et al. [25]	Automotive	● I ○	○ I ●
Ohki et al. [38]	Field	● I ○	● I ○
Oniga et al. [12]	Automotive	○ I ●	● I ○
Papadakis et al. [9]	Search and rescue	● I ○	● I ○
Pfaff et al. [37]	Natural	● I ○	● I ○
Rohmer et al. [47]	Planetary	● I ○	● I ○
Roccacio et al. [7]	Natural	○ I ●	● I ○
Suger et al. [11]	Natural	● I ○	○ I ●
Thruh et al. [16]	Automotive	● I ○	○ I ●
Vandapel et al. [39]	Natural	○ I ●	○ I ●
Whitty et al. [40]	Field	● I ○	○ I ●

The full bullet indicates the classification.

Table 1. Comparison of the literature, the table classifies space representations and used sensors for traversability purposes

This analysis suggests that both DEMs and point clouds are used for traversability analysis; however, one can consider as a possible trend, the use of point clouds for terrain traversability, since recent researches are going towards this direction. Contrary, DEMs constitute a stable and robust tool, widely used in all the fields of robotics, and it is even possible to find recent extensions of research. To cite one of them, in [38], the authors use an extended elevation models as improvement to DEMs. The historical predominant application of traversability is in natural outdoor environments, where the assumptions of surface regularity cannot be applied. Only recently, the study of surfaces is gaining interest in the automotive sector, in which all researches are quite recent, since this technology was never required in the field. Possible uses are as follows: pavement distress detection [41], sidewalk detection [12], or segment terrain's inliers and outliers to be used for obstacles detection [13].

From sensors point of view, laser scanner are commonly used for specific applications such as planetary or search and rescue, whereas stereocameras are preferred in applications where the cost-effectiveness of cameras can be attractive. However, it is important to cite that ToF sensors are commonly used for geometry-based traversability techniques, whereas cameras are used in the case of appearance-based classification.

3. Terrain traversability analysis

From a dictionary definition, the word "traversability" denotes *"the condition of being traversable"* and traversable concerns the capability *"to travel across or through."*[1] This linguistic definition does not explicitly refer to means; for instance, if one is conducting a car the word traversable better characterizes the action of "driving across or through," whereas going by feet may refer to the natural process of "walking across or through." However, an allusion to two elements exists in the definition: (i) the space, to be traversed, and (ii) the mean, to traverse the space. In classical control theory, such elements are expressed using concepts such as controllability or reachability, and they are related to the properties of a system to reach a generic state from the origin or the other way round, according to a specific physical model of the process. Whereas a thorough survey on traversability assessment suggests that its formal definition is still missing in the robotic community [6]. In the same survey, a qualitative definition of traversability in the context of UGVs appears, stating:

> *"The capability of a ground vehicle to reside over a terrain region under an admissible state wherein it is capable of entering given its current state, this capability being quantified by taking into account a terrain model, the robotic vehicle model, the kinematic constraints of the vehicle and a set of criteria based on which the optimality of an admissible state can be assessed [6]."*

Though descriptive and valuable, this definition only provides ingredients to reach a more general and formal definition of traversability. First of all, it is important to consider few

[1] Definition from Oxford Dictionaries.

aspects: (i) a robot model including its motion constraints, (ii) space representation, for example, the terrain model, and (iii) a set of criteria to express the traversability properties. All these concepts will be later recalled.

Since this topic is attracting further researches, a more general definition of traversability is given later by Cafaro et al. [43]. The authors have made a valuable work on the theory of space description using point clouds, introducing the definitions of *traversable region* and *traversability map* in the context of graph theory, thus defining traversability as the existence of a connection (i.e., a branch) between two vertexes of a graph. A different characterization in terms of fuzzy sets was already provided by Seraji [48], and even though it was not general, the author distinguishes among different types of terrain providing the introduction of this topic in the robotic community. In the light of all relevant works made in research a clear discrepancy between theory and application appears. This section will attempt to fill this gap, using the elements in the literature to reach a definition in terms of control space which can consider the robot model, its operating environment and an evaluation criterion.

3.1. Robot models and configuration space

Prom the basis of control theory, it is well known that the robot control includes three different, but fundamental, items: process, controller, and sensors. This concept perfectly describes the ancient meaning of the word *control,* which refers to the capacity of inducing a specific behavior to a process based on observations of its evolution. Starting from simple regulators, the control theory evolved towards robot control, regarding robots considered as complex processes. Obviously, as processes complexity increases, the complexity of controllers increases itself. The reason of the growing complexity of robotic systems is furthermore referred to the requirement of a higher level of interaction between robots and real world.

The physical description of robots in control theory typically is expressed through a process and a state space. Thus, given the state $x \in X$, where $X \subset \mathbb{R}^n$ is referred to as *state space,* and the command $u \in U$ with $U \subset \mathbb{R}^m$, called *command space,* a discrete system can be defined as:

$$x(k+1) = f(x(k), u(k)) \quad f: \mathbb{R}^n \to \mathbb{R}^n. \tag{7}$$

The function *f*, referred to as *transition function,* denotes the behavior of a system, from simple systems to complex mobile robots. The generality of this definition expresses the evolution of any physical process and though usable in any possible situation, its elements, including space structures and transition function, must be explicitly expressed in practical applications. The command space can be easily defined given the kinematic/dynamic properties of the robot and its actuators, and it can be considered as a finite set of possible actions. Whereas the state space may be uncountable, open set and even featuring time-variant elements (e.g., moving obstacles); as a consequence, it deserves a specific description.

For the sake of clarity, let us mention an example, the state space for a planar vehicle may be defined as $X = \mathbb{R}^2 \times SO(2)$ denoting $\mathbb{R}^2$ the translations on x and y axis, respectively, and $SO(2)$

the rotation around the axis orthogonal to the motion plane, also known as $SE(2)$, special Euclidean group. This state space constitutes an open and uncountable set. Considering the 3D space, it is also common to find the state space as $SE(3) = \mathbb{R}^3 \times SO(3)$ referring to 3D translations and rotations, for example, in the case of position and orientation of UAVs (unmanned aerial vehicles) or even simply the end effector's pose in manipulators. Talking about traversability and driving on not-flat terrains, the use of 3D representation is also becoming common for a more accurate design of autonomous navigation systems for UGVs. As a general definition, in robotics, it is possible to find the name *configuration space* $\mathcal{C}$ or simply C-Space [49, 50] describing the set of all possible configurations of the robot. C-Space refers to a broad family of constructions closely related to the *state space* notion in physics which is common in general control theory.

Now, let us suppose that the C-Space contains a forbidden region $\mathcal{O} \subset \mathcal{C}$; moreover, since the mobile robot will also live in C-Space, we can denote the robot geometry as a subset $\mathcal{M} \subset \mathcal{C}$, all sets may be expressed using polygonal or polyhedral models. At this point, let us denote as $q \in \mathcal{C}$ a possible configuration of our mobile robot $\mathcal{M}$, as a result $\mathcal{M}(q)$ is the configuration of the entire robot geometry in C-Space, note that in the case of $SE(2)$, the configuration of the robot at the time k will be $q = (x_k, y_k, \theta_k)$. Under the aforementioned assumptions, an *obstacle region* can be expressed as follows:

$$\mathcal{C}_{obs} = \{q \in \mathcal{C} \mid \mathcal{M}(q) \cap \mathcal{O} \neq \emptyset\} \subseteq \mathcal{C}. \tag{8}$$

The obstacle region constitutes the set of all robot's configurations $\mathcal{M}(q)$ intersecting the forbidden subspace. All the other configurations can be denoted as *free space*, $\mathcal{C}_{free}$, and obviously $\mathcal{C}_{free} = \mathcal{C} \backslash \mathcal{C}_{obs}$. Let us note that the sets $\mathcal{O}, \mathcal{M}$ and $\mathcal{C}_{obs}$ must be closed set in $\mathcal{C}$, as a consequence $\mathcal{C}_{free}$ must be open, this will ensure the possibility to formalize an optimization problem in $\mathcal{C}_{free}$; moreover, it ensures that the robot can drive arbitrary close to an obstacle without colliding it. As last consideration, though different in the formulation, the configuration q and the state x in Eq. (7) may be considered similar; as a consequence, there exists a transition function to go from a configuration q_1 at a time t_1, to another configuration q_2 at the time t_2. A rough analogy between *states* and *configurations* suggests that the transition function can be expressed as $q_{k+1} = f(q_k, u_k)$; clearly defining the robot $\mathcal{M}$ in the configuration q moving according to the equation of motion f.

This discussion does not pretend to be a complete description of spaces and sets, but it only gives the preliminary knowledge for the reading of this text, for additional details about assumptions, demonstrations, and definitions please refer to [50] as a relevant reference in the field.

The reason of the diffusion of C-Spaces in robotics research resides in the possibility of describing them as manifolds, i.e., topological spaces that behave at every point like our intuitive notion of a surface, and the best way of describing the terrain is to consider its topological properties. Hence, considering a ground vehicle, the configuration space cannot be other than the terrain region it is driving on, described as a manifold.

3.2. Traversability characterization

The previous theory considers the robot moving in a configuration space $\mathcal{C}$ composed by a free space part $\mathcal{C}_{free}$ and a forbidden region $\mathcal{O}$. Yet, considering the concept of traversability as the condition of being traversable, then it is simple to understand that the free space can be considered as traversable, while the forbidden space may be not traversable. This definition would be perfectly enough for a binary classification of traversability.

Nevertheless, we are looking for a more general definition; thus, the traversability can be seen as the capability to travel across of through, which implies that the aforementioned binary definition could be extended. Indeed, the set could be forbidden (i.e., not traversable at all) or partially forbidden (i.e., traversable with some grade of membership). This clearly recalls the fuzzy logic[2] that can be considered as an extension of the binary logic, such that statements need not be true or false, but they may have a grade of truth between 0 and 1. As a result, one can suppose the existence of a fuzzy set defined following.

Definition 1 *Let be given a robot* $\mathcal{M}(q)$ *expressed as a closed subset* $\mathcal{M} \subset \mathcal{C}$ *where* $q \in \mathcal{C}$ *is a possible configuration of the mobile robot* $\mathcal{M}$*, and* $\mathcal{C}$ *denotes its C-Space. Let us suppose the existence of a not empty free space* $\mathcal{C}_{free} \subset \mathcal{C}$*, with* $\mathcal{C}_{free} \neq \emptyset$*. Moreover, let us suppose be defined a traversability function* $\mathcal{T} : \mathcal{C}_{free} \rightarrow [0, 1]$*, the traversable region will, be the defined by the following fuzzy set:*

$$\mathcal{C}_{tr} = \left\{ (q \in \mathcal{C}_{free}, \mathcal{T}(q)) \mid \mathcal{M}(q) \in \mathcal{C}_{free} \right\}. \tag{9}$$

First of all, let us note that the traversable set is included into the C-Space by definition, $\mathcal{C}_{tr} \subseteq \mathcal{C}$, because the membership function $\mathcal{T}$ is defined in $\mathcal{C}_{free} \subset \mathcal{C}$; moreover $q \in \mathcal{C}_{free}$ and also $\mathcal{M}(q) \in \mathcal{C}_{free}$. The traversability function used in this definition can be considered as a clear analogous of the more general membership functions which are common in the theory of fuzzy sets. As a result, when $\mathcal{T}$ goes to 1 the statement "is traversale" will be true, whereas if $\mathcal{T} \rightarrow 0$ the statement "is traversable" will be false.

The aforementioned definition considers all the elements previously indicated, i.e., a robot model $\mathcal{M}$, a space structure $\mathcal{C}$ and a set of traversability criteria $\mathcal{T}$. The use of this definition, according to an explicit expression of $\mathcal{T}$, can also be used to solve optimal control problems.

In order to better clarify the concept, **Figure 3** expresses the difference between a simple occupancy map in **Figure 3a**, where free space and obstacles are clearly distinguished through a binary classification black/white, whereas the concept of fuzzy set in **Figure 3b** better characterizes the terrain according to the membership function $\mathcal{T}$. Its values are expressed

---

[2] Definition of fuzzy set: Given a generic set X and a membership function $f: X \rightarrow [0; 1]$, the fuzzy set A is defined as $A = \{(x, f(x)) | x \in X\}$.

according to a degree of membership in gray scale, denoting in white high values of $\mathcal{T}$; on the contrary, black corresponds to low values of $\mathcal{T}$. The presence of the region A in **Figure 3b** can be interpreted as a region "less-traversable" than usual, but still not classifiable as an obstacle, a politic of driving control may generate safe plans.

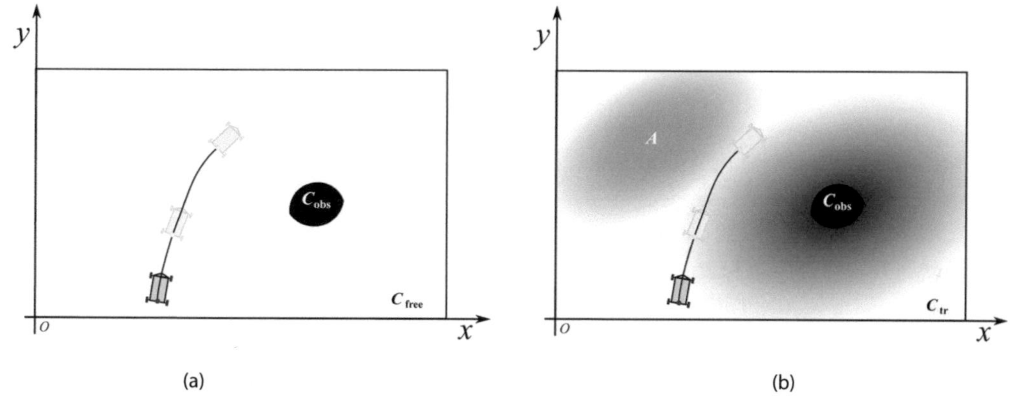

Figure 3. Depiction of the free space and fuzzy traversability characterization, the entire area inside the rectangle can be considered as C_{free} in (a), whereas the gray-scale gradient indicates the value of the membership function $\mathcal{T}$ for each point of C_{tr} in (b). The presence of the region A denotes a portion of the free space featuring different values of traversability.

4. Discussion

As the definition of traversability previously introduced can be of general value for geometry-based terrain analysis purposes, how to use it in order to build practical traversability functions will be following shown, including the re-definition of classical methods, such as elevation models and roughness models. The exposed examples cover both binary classification methods and cost-based assessment methods. Along the discussion, an irregular terrain model in the form of a DEM of about 20 m × 20 m, featuring a 0.25m grid size, has been used in order to compare different methods. Let us note that the terrain model, considered as sample model, expressed as a DEM is stored into a 80 × 80 size matrix, that is, 6400 elements. The same data in form of a point cloud, storing only the points' Cartesian coordinates, will take 6400 × 3 points. This clearly demonstrates the advantage in handling DEMs instead of point clouds; however, using DEMs part of the information is lost due to the assumption of terrain regularity, which is not always applicable. Moreover, ToF sensors as well as stereocamera triangulation always provide a set of distances between the cameras and sampled points in the space, that is, a point cloud, thus a transformation is required, including its computational cost, to build the digital map.

4.1. Binary classification for traversability

Let us consider the example of a binary classification and apply the aforementioned definition to find a member function $\mathcal{T}$ such that the traversability region corresponds to the free part of the configuration space. Given a generic robot $\mathcal{M}$, in the configuration space $\mathcal{C}$, in this simple case $\mathcal{T}$ can be expressed by the function:

$$\mathcal{T} = \begin{cases} \mathcal{T}(q) = 1 & \forall q \in \mathcal{C} | \mathcal{M}(q) \subseteq \mathcal{C}_{free} \\ \mathcal{T}(q) = 0 & \forall q \in \mathcal{C} | \mathcal{M}(q) \cap \mathcal{C}_{obs} \neq \emptyset \end{cases} \tag{10}$$

Note that, even though this function is the simplest possible, it works regardless of the particular structure of the C-Space, and it converges into the general theory of configuration space. However, in practical cases, it is expected the free space to be explicitly expressed. To prove that $\mathcal{C}_{tr} \subseteq \mathcal{C}_{free}$ is true in the case of binary classification, let us consider that by definition that $\mathcal{C}_{tr} \subseteq \mathcal{C}_{free}$. As a result, the only part that should be proven is $\mathcal{C}_{tr} \subseteq \mathcal{C}_{free}$, if $\mathcal{T}$ is defined as in Eq. (10). Hence, let us suppose that exists a configuration q_k such that $q \in \mathcal{C}_{free}$ but $q_k \notin \mathcal{C}_{tr}$. This implies $\mathcal{T}(q_k) = 0$; hence, $\mathcal{M}(q_k) \cap \mathcal{C}_{obs} \neq \emptyset$, but this is absurd because q_k would belong to both $\mathcal{C}_{free}$ and $\mathcal{C}_{obs}$. As a result, $\mathcal{C}_{tr} = \mathcal{C}_{free}$ if $\mathcal{T}$ is defined as in Eq. (10).

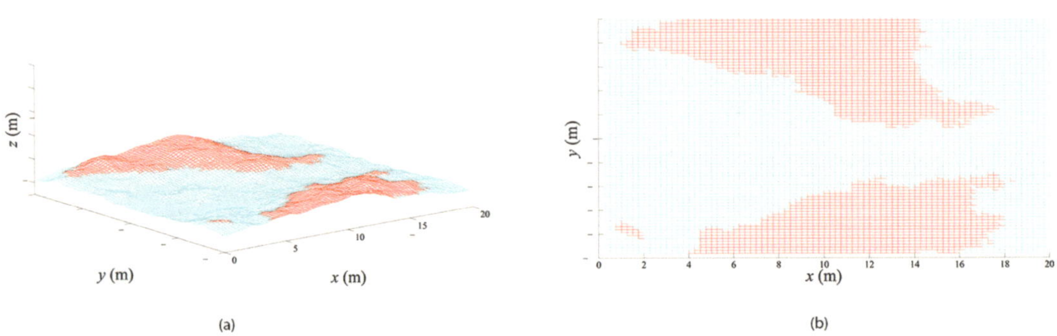

Figure 4. Binary traversability rule applied on an elevation model. In (a) and (b) the 3D-view and xy-view are shown. The red color labels not traversable regions (i.e., $\mathcal{T} = 0$), whereas the cyan color denotes the traversable parts of the terrain, $\mathcal{T} = 1$.

As an example of functionality, **Figure 4** presents a binary classification applied to a sample terrain model. For the sake of the example, given $q = (x,y,z)$, $\mathcal{C}_{free}$ has been defined as the set of points such that $|z| \leq z_{max}$. The result is a cyan region which can be considered as traversable, that is, belonging to $\mathcal{C}_{free}$, and a red region which can be considered as not traversable, that is, $\notin \mathcal{C}_{free}$. The example explicitly refers to the 3D space; however, the definition in Eq. (10) has general value, since the structure of the configuration space has not been explicitly given. Though simple and widely used this method neglects information about intermediate levels of elevation or local irregularities; hence, it is much more used in indoor structured environ-

http://dx.doi.org/10.5772/64489

ments where there are strong discontinuities (e.g., floor, walls) and under the assumption of regular flat floor surface. A different way to see this concept consists in the occupancy maps, which consider a cell as not traversable, if its elevation is higher than a threshold, that is, obstacle.

4.2. Elevation terrain model for traversability

Typically used in mobile robotics, elevation models may be described using the formulation in Eq. (9). Let us suppose to have a ground vehicle that can move in three-dimensional space. As indicated earlier, its configuration space can be expressed as $\mathcal{C} = \mathbb{R}^3$, neglecting the orientation terms to simplify the notation, the ground vehicle may be considered as a subset $\mathcal{M} \subset \mathcal{C}$, and we can also consider the existence of a forbidden region $\mathcal{O} \subset \mathcal{C}$. Now, let us construct a traversability function given a terrain model expressed as follows:

$$\mathcal{C}_{free} = \{q(x,y,z) \in \mathcal{C} \mid \mathcal{M}(q) \cap \mathcal{O} = \varnothing\}, \tag{11}$$

where $z = g(x,y)$, with $g: \mathbb{R}^2 \rightarrow \mathbb{R}$ supposed to be regular; moreover, x and y are considered as limited, thus $|x| \leq x_{max}$, $|y| \leq y_{max}$. In this way, a bounded portion of the x, y plane has been defined. As a result, given a generic shaped robot $\mathcal{M}$ in the configuration space $\mathcal{C}$, a traversability function $\mathcal{T}$ that considers an elevation terrain model can be expressed by the following:

$$\mathcal{T}(q) = 1 - \left| \frac{z_q}{z_{max}} \right| \quad \forall q \in \mathcal{C}_{tr}, z_{max} \neq 0 \mid \mathcal{M}(q) \subset \mathcal{C}_{free}. \tag{12}$$

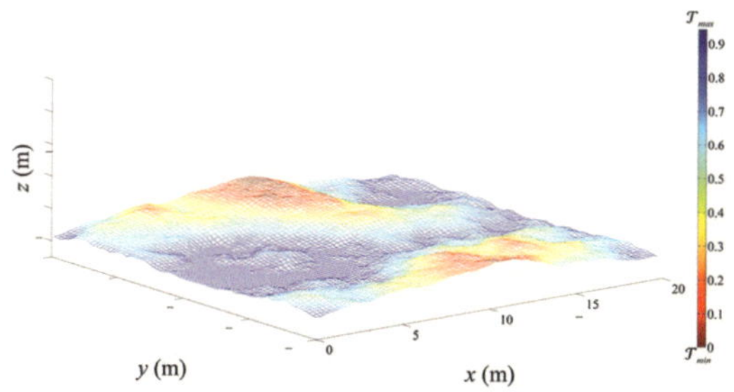

(a)

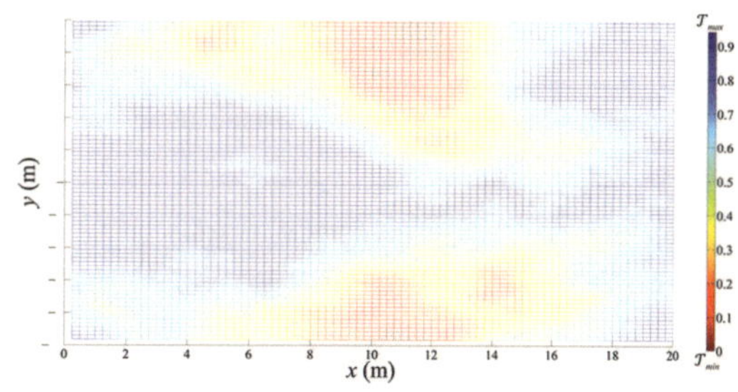

(b)

Figure 5. The elevation model better describes the sample terrain in **Figure 4**, the higher informative content allows to perform better cost-based traversability analysis, in (a) the 3D mesh is presented, whereas the xy-axis view is depicted in (b).

One should note that in Eq. (12) if $z_q \rightarrow z_{max}$ then $\mathcal{T} = 0$ and the configuration will fall into low values of membership function and this implies that the point will not belong to $\mathcal{C}_{free}$. However, even though the configuration of the robot includes orientation angles in its formalization, this traversability function does not consider any orientation in its values and this results in a limitation in the practical application of pure elevation-based methods. For the sake of completeness, we should consider the case of $z_{max} \to \infty$, where $\mathcal{T} = 1 \, \forall z_q$, but this case can be considered as trivial.

The example of this type of analysis is reported in **Figure 5**, where the values of $\mathcal{T}$ are indicated as a color bar from blue corresponding to traversable regions, to red denoting not-traversable part of terrain. It results evident that a control rule based on such analysis will bring the robot towards the lowest regions of the terrain, which though reasonable, it may be not the best behavior according to the objective of the robot movements. Let us observe that in this method, the robot shape is considered as a single point in the calculation of the traversability function, hence considering only the terrain elevation.

4.3. Traversability model based on roughness index

A widely used approach, for geometry and cost-based terrain traversability analysis, consists in the definition of the roughness index [47]. It is defined as the standard deviation of the elevation values in a specific region of the terrain, given by the projection of the robot shape on the ground.

Given a terrain region considered as free space $\mathcal{C}_{free}$, defined as in Eq. (11), and a robot model $\mathcal{M}$ described using any polygonal model. Then, it is possible to define the roughness index B_q of the terrain, when the robot is in the configuration $q \in \mathcal{C}_{free}$ as the standard deviation of the elevation values Z_q of the surface given by the intersection between $\mathcal{M}(q)$ and $\mathcal{C}_{free}$.

$$B_q = \sqrt{E(Z_q - \mu)^2}, \tag{13}$$

where $Z_q = \{p \in \mathcal{C}_{free} \cap \mathcal{M}(q)\} \neq \emptyset$ is the set of all points that fall into the intersection between the robot $\mathcal{M}(q)$ and the free space, and $\mu = E(Z_q)$ is the average of the elevation values in the same region. Since the values of B_q are not limited in [0, 1] the traversability function related to the roughness index, according to the definition in Eq. (9), may be considered using a normalization as following:

$$\mathcal{T}(q) = 1 - \frac{B_q}{B_{max}} \quad \forall q \in \mathcal{C}, B_{max} \neq 0 \mid \mathcal{M}(q) \subset \mathcal{C}_{free}. \tag{14}$$

As in the previous case, Eq. (14) $\to 0$ if $B_q \to B_{max}$ and the configuration q will fall into low values of membership function and this implies that it does not belong to $\mathcal{C}_{free}$. Moreover,

$B_q \geq 0 \implies \frac{B_q}{B_{max}} \in [0,1]$, as a result $\mathcal{T}(q)$ is well defined. Also in this case, if $B_{max} \to \infty$, $\mathcal{T} = 1 \, \forall B_q$ can be considered as trivial.

Figure 6 shows an example of traversability map obtained using the roughness index, for the sake of this calculation, the robot has been considered to cover an area of about 8 × 8 cells of the map having grid size of 0.25 m, corresponding to 2 meters in size. The consideration of the standard deviation on a terrain region calculated according to the robot's geometry may be considered as a robust method and, for this reason, widely used for practical applications. One should note that between the pure elevation traversability analysis and the roughness analysis, a specific region of the terrain appears as irregular and dangerous, corresponding to a local surface minimum. This evaluation agrees with the reality that a robot may get stuck into a hole. On the contrary, the same analysis does not mark as irregular the peak of the hill that may be perfectly traversable as upland. However, it is clear that also this method may fail in the simple case of a surface featuring a slope, which though regular and traversable, it may present high values of variance in its elevation [51].

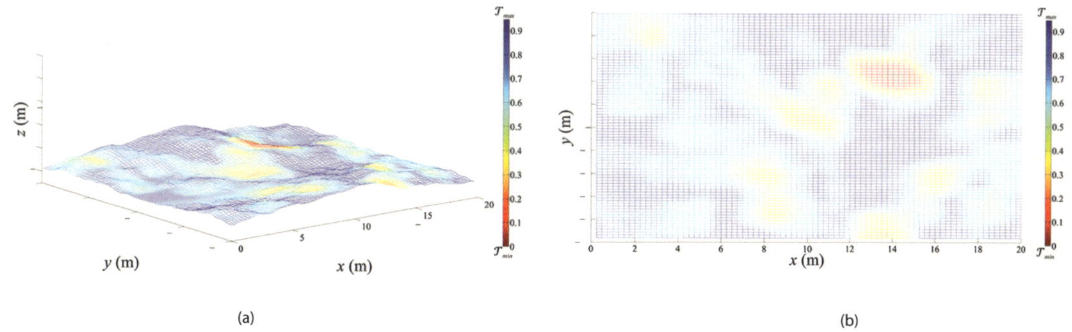

Figure 6. Roughness traversability analysis result based on the roughness index in Eq. (13), integrated into the membership function in Eq. (14); (a) 3D surface model; (b) xy-view. The color bar indicates increasing values of traversability, where red corresponds to not traversable regions, while blue corresponds to traversable portion of terrain.

4.4. Unevenness point descriptor-based model

As an alternative analysis to solve the problems related to the variance of the elevation in sloped regular surfaces, the use of normal vectors to estimate surface irregularities was presented in [27], where the authors defined the unevenness point descriptor (UPD), as a simple choice to extract traversability information from 3D point cloud data. Specifically, the UPD describes surfaces using a normal analysis in a neighborhood, resulting in an efficient description of both irregularities and inclination.

Summarizing the concept, let $\mathcal{P}$ be a point cloud, that is, a set of points defined by their Cartesian coordinates defined as in Eq. (3), and let p^q be a given point defined as the *query point*. The neighborhood of p^q in $\mathcal{P}$ can be defined as in Eq. (4), given a search radius $d_m > 0$. Then, we define the unevenness point descriptor F_U in p^q, as: $F_U(p^q, P^q) = \{\vec{r}^q, \zeta^q\}$, where $\vec{r}^q = (r^q_x, r^q_y, r^q_z)$

is given by the vector sum of all the vectors $\vec{n}_i$ normal vectors in the neighbors P^q, that is, $\vec{r}^q = \sum_{i=1}^{k} \vec{n}_i$ with $i = 1,...,k$, ζ^q is defined by $\zeta^q = |\vec{r}^q|/k$, and k is the number of elements in P^q.

The components of $\vec{r}^q$ provide information about the global direction of the local surface in the sensor reference frame. Whereas ζ^q can be interpreted as a local inverse "unevenness index," since it assesses the degree of local roughness, and it depends on the distribution of the direction of the normal vectors in the neighborhood. ζ^q is normalized by k, i.e., the number of points in P^q; hence, it is possible to compare the unevenness index of different points among each other. The main advantages of this descriptor reside in its simplicity and robustness for traversability evaluation. Contrary to other methods, UPD detects the variations in the surface orientation instead of the variation of the pure elevation, which leads to a general description of regularity in the surface. Moreover, the UPD can be easily adapted to the robot's specific task by appropriately setting the neighborhood size, d_m. In practice, its value is fixed at the beginning of the operations based on the robot geometric size [26]. As further observation, given a neighborhood P^q denoting a certain region of the terrain, its orientation can be written as follows:

$$\theta(P^q) = \cos^{-1}\left(\frac{r_z^q}{|\vec{r}^q|}\right), \tag{15}$$

where r_z^q represents the third component of $\vec{r}^q$, orthogonal to the xy-plane, as a consequence, $d(P^q)$ represents the global orientation of the surface portion P^q respect to the plane xy.

To bring the unevenness index into the definition of a traversable region, we can consider as given the C-Space $\mathcal{C}$ and a forbidden space $\mathcal{O} \subset \mathcal{C}$, then a free space can be defined as in the following Eq. (16):

$$\mathcal{C}_{free} = \{q \in \mathcal{C} \cap \mathcal{P} \mid \mathcal{M}(q) \cap \mathcal{O} \neq \varnothing\}, \tag{16}$$

where $\mathcal{P}$ is a generic portion of space expressed as a point cloud. Let us note that the meaning of the intersection with $\mathcal{P}$ consists in a practical limitation of the C-Space in the part the robot can see or has information about. Then, let us suppose to be given the unevenness index $\zeta^q \ \forall p^q \in \mathcal{P}$, the traversability region may be identified by the set in Eq. (9), where the membership function is given by the following:

$$\mathcal{T}(q) = 1 - \zeta^q \quad \forall q \in \mathcal{C} \mid \mathcal{M}(q) \subset \mathcal{C}_{free}. \tag{17}$$

http://dx.doi.org/10.5772/64489

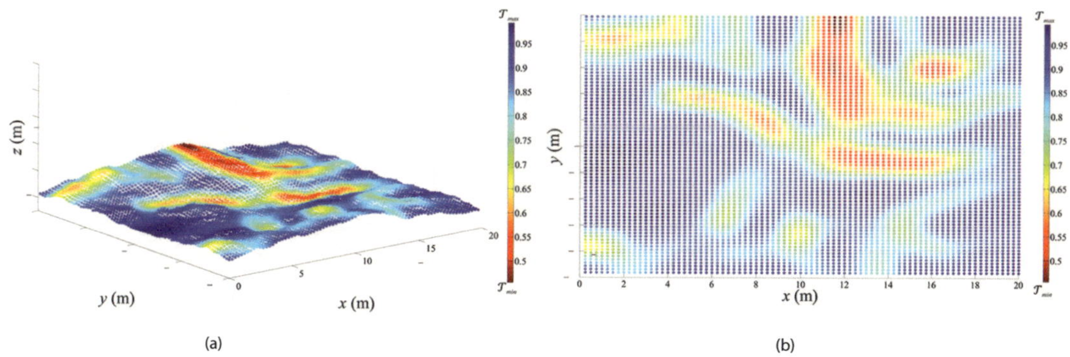

Figure 7. Unevenness point descriptor-based model for geometric traversability analysis applied on a point cloud depicting the sample terrain model. In (a) and (b), the 3D view and xy-view, respectively, are depicted. The search radius for the UPD calculation is $d_m = 1\ m$.

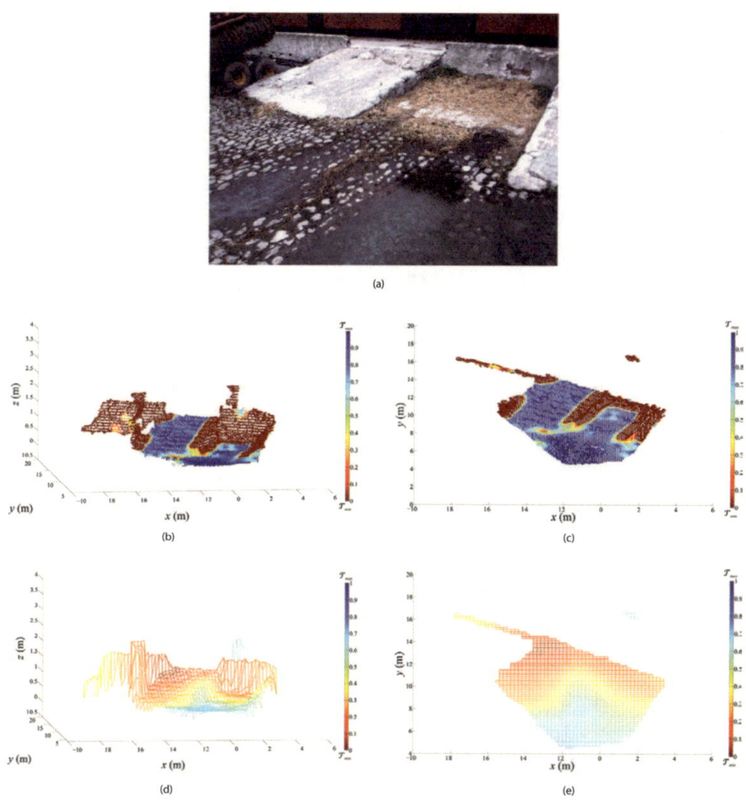

Figure 8. UPD point-descriptor analysis. In (b) the 3D point cloud is shown using the color bar to denote traversability value, whereas its relative xy-view is shown in (c). As the point cloud has been obtained by stereo-triangulation, the left-camera image is shown in (a). The roughness index-based analysis in Eq. (14) produces poor results on the same scenario using a DEM approach, see 3D-view (d) and xy-view (e).

Now, let us observe that in its original form the UPD considers the robot model into the parameter $d_{m'}$ at least in its size, that has been said to be fixed at the beginning of robot operations, according to its shape. However, it is possible to generalize the concept of neighborhood P^q considering the set of points which fall in the set not as a sphere neighborhood but as the intersection between a polyhedral robot model $\mathcal{M}$ and the free part of C-Space, hence $P^q = \{p \in \mathcal{C}_{free} \cap \mathcal{M}(p^q)\} \neq \emptyset$ This generalization allows the user to better define the robot shape into the descriptor.

The example of the UPD analysis, for the same terrain model considered as sample, is reported in **Figure 7**, for the sake of visibility, the values of ζ^q have been normalized to their minimum values in the region, since the results of variation were close to regularity. During the calculation, the search radius has been set to 1 m, according to the previous example of the roughness index. Contrary to the previous approaches, in the UPD analysis, the strong variations such as the depressions are now considered as not regular showing a different perception of the traversability of this terrain model.

As last example, in **Figure 8**, the UPD has been applied on a point cloud obtained by triangulation on a stereocamera in real environment, the value of the traversabilitv function is reported using in color scale, whereas the left-camera image of the scenario is reported in **Figure 8a**. This scene has been extracted from a dataset thoroughly analyzed in [51]. It can be interesting to note that the presented case scenario features a ramp to access an indoor structure. The ramp is considered as regular via UPD analysis, whereas it may be misinterpreted considering elevation model as well as the roughness index. All the borders are correctly detected as not traversable regions. As the matter of fact, **Figure 8d** and **Figure 8e** present the same scenario described using a DEM and the traversability function in Eq. (14). The misunderstanding of the scenario leads to the erroneous classification of the ramp to access the building behind it as fully not traversable. On the contrary, in **Figure 8b** and **Figure 8c** the scene is properly interpreted using the UPD approach.

5. Conclusion and further extensions

Along the chapter, different methods of geometry-based traversability for mobile robotics have been explored. A thorough review on the topic suggests that the future trend of sensors and space description for traversability purposes will refer to point clouds and time-of-flight sensors, or stereo-3D reconstruction. The necessity to improve the description of terrain, removing the assumption of regularity, will bring the robot towards the full 3D reconstruction of the environment at least in short range visibility. Among different methods analyzed in the discussion, the UPD has demonstrated highest capability of recognition even though it could be costly in terms of computational performances. The contributions in this work are as follows: (i) a review of the field with comparison among technologies, (ii) a new definition of traversability that can be of general value for robot navigation purposes, and (iii) a comparison among literature methods including practical examples.

To conclude this chapter, it is worth to give some possible extensions of this work and future developments. One of them could be the definition of traversable regions in terms of probability. Indeed, it should be possible to include a probability function in terms of risk-of-collision or probability of traverse, in which high values refer to minimum probability of collision (i.e., max traversing probability) or low values imply maximum probability of collision (i.e., min traversing probability). Moreover, the traversability regions as defined during this chapter may fit for navigation purposes using the common potential fields, where the potential function will consider traversable regions as "attractive." On the contrary, "repulsive" regions will coincide with low values of traversability function. Literature in this field typically considers potential functions that use the distance from obstacles instead of a complete traversability description.

Author details

Mauro Bellone

Address all correspondence to: bellonemauro@gmail.com

Department of Applied Mechanics, Chalmers University of Technology, Gothenburg, Sweden

References

[1] *Automated Guided Vehicle Market by Type – Global Forecast to 2020.* Marketsandmarkets, 2015.

[2] J. Greenough, *The self-driving car report: forecasts, tech timelines, and the benefits and barriers that will impact adoption.* BI Intelligence, 2015.

[3] H. A. Yanco, A. Norton, W. Ober, D. Shane, A. Skinner, and J. Vice, "Analysis of human-robot interaction at the darpa robotics challenge trials," *Journal of Field Robotics,* vol. 32, no. 3, pp. 420–444, 2015.

[4] Ellery, A. (2015). "Planetary Rovers: Robotic Exploration of the Solar System". Springer, ISBN: 978–3–642–03258–5.

[5] M. H. Hebert, C. E. Thorpe, and A. Stentz, "Intelligent unmanned ground vehicles: autonomous navigation research at Carnegie Mellon" (Vol. 388). Springer Science & Business Media, Eds. 2012, ISBN:1461563259.

[6] P. Papadakis, "Terrain traversability analysis methods for unmanned ground vehicles: A survey," *Engineering Applications of Artificial Intelligence,* vol. 26, no. 4, pp. 1373–1385, 2013.

[7] H. Roncancio, M. Becker, A. Broggi, and S. Cattani, "Traversability analysis using terrain mapping and online-trained terrain type classifier," in *Intelligent Vehicles Symposium Proceedings, 2014 IEEE,* pp. 1239–1244, IEEE, 2014.

[8] S. Thrun, "Learning occupancy grid maps with forward sensor models," *Autonomous Robots,* vol. 15, no. 2, pp. 111–127, 2003.

[9] P. Papadakis, F. Pirri "3D Mobility Learning and Regression of Articulated, Tracked Robotic Vehicles by Physics–based Optimization" International conference on Virtual Reality Interaction and Physical Simulation, Eurographics, Dec 2012, Darmstadt, Germany.

[10] Y. Tanaka, Y. Ji, A. Yamashita, and H. Asama, "Fuzzy based traversability analysis for a mobile robot on rough terrain," in *Proceedings of the 2015 IEEE International Conference on Robotics and Automation,* 2015.

[11] B. Suger, B. Steder, and W. Burgard, "Traversability analysis for mobile robots in outdoor environments: A semi-supervised learning approach based on 3d-lidar data," in *Robotics and Automation (ICRA), 2015 IEEE International Conference on,* pp. 3941-3946, 2015.

[12] F. Oniga and S. Nedevschi, "Processing dense stereo data using elevation maps: Road surface, traffic isle, and obstacle detection," *IEEE Transactions on Vehicular Technology,* vol. 59, pp. 1172–1182, 2010.

[13] A. Broggi, E. Cardarelli, S. Cattani, and M. Sabbatelli, "Terrain mapping for off-road autonomous ground vehicles using rational b-spline surfaces and stereo vision," in *Intelligent Vehicles Symposium (IV), 2013 IEEE,* pp. 648–653, 2013.

[14] K. Dongshin, M. O. Sang, and M. R. James, "Traversability classification for ugv navigation: A comparison of patch and superpixel representations," (San Diego, CA), pp. 3166-3173, International Conference on Intelligent Robots and Systems, 2007.

[15] A. Howard and H. Saraji, "Vision-based terrain characterization and traversability assessment," *Journal of Robotic System,* vol. 18, no. 10, pp. 77–587, 2001.

[16] S. Thrun, M. Montemerlo, and A. Aron, "Probabilistic Terrain Analysis For High–Speed Desert Driving" In Robotics: Science and Systems, pp. 16–19, Philadelphia, USA, August 2006.

[17] M. Häselich, M. Arends, N. Wojke, F. Neuhaus, and D. Paulus, "Probabilistic terrain classification in unstructured environments," *Robotics and Autonomous Systems,* vol. 61, no. 10, pp. 1051–1059, 2013.

[18] K. Iagnemma, H. Shibly, and S. Dubowsky, "On-line terrain parameter estimation for planetary rovers," in *Robotics and Automation, 2002. Proceedings. ICRA '02. IEEE International Conference on,* vol. 3, pp. 3142–3147, IEEE, 2002.

[19] E. Coyle and E. G. E. Jr., "A comparison of classifier performance for vibration-based terrain classification," tech. rep., DTIC Document, 2008.

[20] F. L. G. Bermudez, C. J. Ryan, D. W. Haldane, P. Abbeel, and R. S. Fearing, "Performance analysis and terrain classification for a legged robot over rough terrain," in *Intelligent Robots and Systems (IROS), 2012 IEEE/RSJ International Conference on*, pp. 513–519, IEEE, 2012.

[21] R. B. Rusu, Semantic 3D Object Maps for Everyday Manipulation in Human Living Environments. Künstl Intell (2010) 24: 345. doi:10.1007/s13218–010–0059–6.

[22] M. Bellone and G. Reina, "Pavement distress detection and avoidance for intelligent vehicles", International Journal of Vehicle Autonomous Systems, 2016, Vol. 14, ISSN: 1471–0226.

[23] J. D. S. Prince, "Computer Vision: Models, Learning, and Inference" Cambridge University Press, 1st ed., 2012.

[24] R. Szeliski, "Computer Vision: Algorithm and applications" Springer, 2010, ISBN1848829353.

[25] F. Neuhaus, D. Dillenberger, J. Pellenz and D. Paulus, "Terrain drivability analysis in 3D laser range data for autonomous robot navigation in unstructured environments," 2009 IEEE Conference on Emerging Technologies & Factory Automation, Mallorca, Spain, 2009, pp. 1–4, doi: 10.1109/ETFA.2009.5347217.

[26] M. Bellone, A. Messina, and G. Reina, "A new approach for terrain analysis in mobile robot applications," in *Mechatronics (ICM), 2013 IEEE International Conference on*, pp. 225–230, IEEE, 2013.

[27] M. Bellone, G. Reina, N. Giannoccaro, and L. Spedicato, "Unevenness point descriptor for terrain analysis in mobile robot applications," *International Journal of Advanced Robotic Systems*, vol. 10, p. 284, 2013.

[28] J. K. Kearney, X. Yang, and S. Zhang, "Camera calibration using geometric constraints," (San Diego, California, USA), IEEE Computer Society Conference on Computer Vision and Pattern Recognition, 1989.

[29] P. Puget and T. Skordas, "An optimal solution for mobile camera calibration," (Cincinnati, Ohio, USA), IEEE International Conference on Robotics and Automation, 1990.

[30] G. Unal, A. Yezzi, S. Soatto and G. Slabaugh, "A Variational Approach to Problems in Calibration of Multiple Cameras," in IEEE Transactions on Pattern Analysis and Machine Intelligence, vol. 29, no. 8, pp. 1322–1338, Aug. 2007, doi: 10.1109/TPAMI.2007.1035.

[31] L. Heng, B. Li, and M. Pollefeys, "Camodocal: Automatic intrinsic and extrinsic calibration of a rig with multiple generic cameras and odometry," (Tokyo, Japan), International Conference on Intelligent Robots and Systems, 2013.

[32] L. Spedicato, N. I. Giannoccaro, G. Reina, and M. Bellone, "Three different approaches for localization in a corridor environment by means of an ultrasonic wide beam", International Journal of Advanced Robotic Systems, vol. 10, pp. 163–172, March 2013.

[33] J.L. Torres, J.L. Blanco, M. Bellone, F. Rodrìguez, A. Gimènez, and G. Reina – "A proposed software framework aimed at energyefficient autonomous driving of electric vehicles" – International Conference on Simulation, Modeling, and Programming for Autonomous Robots, Bergamo, Italy October 2014, pp. 219–230, ISBN 978–3–319–11899–4;

[34] D. Borrmann, J. Elseberg, K. Lingemann, A. Nüchter, and J. Hertzberg, "Globally consistent 3d mapping with scan matching," *Robotics and Autonomous Systems,* vol. 56, no. 2, pp. 130–142, 2008.

[35] I. S. Kweon and T. Kanade, "High-resolution terrain map from multiple sensor data," *IEEE Transaction on Pattern and Machine Intelligence,* vol. 14, pp. 278–292, 1992.

[36] J. Larson, M. Trivedi, and M. Bruch, "Off-road terrain traversability analysis and hazard avoidance for ugvs," (Baden-Baden, Germany), IEEE Intelligent Vehicles Symposium, 2011.

[37] P. Pfaff, R. Triebel, and W. Burgard, "An efficient extension of elevation maps for outdoor terrain mapping," *In Proceedings of the International Conference on Field and Service Robotics (FSR),* pp. 165–176, 2005.

[38] T. Ohki, K. Nagatani, and K. Yoshida, "Path planning for mobile robot on rough terrain based on sparse transition cost propagation in extended elevation maps," pp. 494–499, 2013 IEEE International Conference on Mechatronics and Automation (ICMA), Aug 2013.

[39] N. Vandapel, D. F. Huber, A. Kapuria, and M. Hebert, "Natural terrain classification using 3-d ladar data," (New Orleans, LA, USA), pp. 5117–5122, IEEE International Conference on Robotics and Automation, 2004.

[40] M. Whitty, S. Cossell, K. S. Dang, J. Guivant, and J. Katupitiya, "Autonomous navigation using a real-time 3d point cloud," in *2010 Australasian Conference on Robotics and Automation,* pp. 1–3, 2010.

[41] M. Bellone and G. Reina, "Road surface analysis for driving assistance," in *Workshop Proceedings of IAS-13 13th International Conference on Intelligent Autonomous Systems Padova (Italy),* pp. 226–234, 2014.

[42] T. Braun, H. Bitsch, and K. Berns, "Visual terrain traversability estimation using a combined slope/elevation model", Advances in Artificial Intelligence Volume 5243 of the series Lecture Notes in Computer Science pp 177–184, Springer, 2008, ISBN 978–3–540–85845–4.

[43] B. Cafaro, M. Gianni, F. Pirri, M. Ruiz, and A. Sinha, "Terrain traversability in rescue environments," in *2013 IEEE International Symposium on Safety, Security, and Rescue Robotics (SSRR)*, pp. 1–8, Oct 2013.

[44] A. Dargazanv and K. Berns, "Stereo-based terrain traversability estimation using surface normals," in *41st International Symposium on Robotics; Proceedings of ISR/Robotik 2014*, pp. 1–7, June 2014.

[45] G. Ishigami, K. Nagatani, and K. Yoshida, "Path planning for planetary exploration rovers and its evaluation based on wheel slip dynamics," in *IEEE International Conference on Robotics and Automation*, pp. 2361–2366, 2007.

[46] T. Kubota, Y. Kuroda, Y. Kunii, and T. Yoshimitsu, "Path planning for newly developed microrover," in *2001. Proceedings 2001 ICRA IEEE International Conference on Robotics and Automation*, vol. 4, pp. 3710–3715, 2001.

[47] E. Rohmer, G. Reina, and K. Yoshida, "Dynamic simulation-based action planner for a reconfigurable hybrid leg-wheel planetary exploration rover," *Advanced Robotics*, vol. 24, no. 8–9, pp. 1219–1238, 2010.

[48] H. Seraji, "Traversability index: A new concept for planetary rovers," (Detroit, MI, USA), pp. 2006–2013, IEEE International Conference on Robotics and Automation, 1999.

[49] J. J. Craig, *Introduction to Robotics: Mechanics and Control*, vol. 3. Pearson Prentice Hall, Upper Saddle River, 2005.

[50] S. M. LaValle "Planning Algorithms" Cambridge University Press, 2006, ISBN1139455176.

[51] M. Bellone, G. Reina, N. Giannoccaro, and L. Spedicato, "3d traversability awareness for rough terrain mobile robots," *Sensor Review*, vol. 34, no. 2, pp. 220–232, 2014.